Praise for *Sacred Celebrations*

In the opening chapter, I was immediately moved to tears as Elizabeth Barbour recounts the final months with her mom before she died. Then, in a later chapter on divorce rituals, I was laughing hysterically envisioning her beating the crap out of her furniture with a tennis racket as she processed the anguish of her divorce. She has a way of bringing you on an emotional journey with her—recounting the highs and lows we all experience through dozens of stories of clients and colleagues as well as sharing her own deeply personal and intimate reflections. Her message is a universal one—we need more ritual in our lives to keep us grounded, centered, and sane to help us make sense of this crazy world. In a world where most of us are living our lives at 100 MPH, Elizabeth reminds us to slow down and honor these sacred transitions in our lives. This is crucial to our healing and allows us to open to the new in our lives. I will be recommending this book to my clients.

Colleen O'Grady
psychotherapist and life coach,
award-winning author of *Dial Down the Drama: Reducing Conflict and Connecting With Your Teenage Daughter* and *Dial Up the Dream: Make Your Daughter's Journey to Adulthood the Best —For Both of You!*

Elizabeth Barbour's one-of-a-kind book *Sacred Celebrations* will inspire you to uplevel how you honor life's joy, losses, and transitions in more meaningful ways, taking them from ordinary, ho-hum, and robotic to extraordinary, memorable, and healing to the core. Every page is power-packed with soul-stirring ideas for every significant life event—the beautiful ones and the toughest. Embracing the importance of ritual and "sacred celebration" in our everyday lives ultimately results in deeper connections, fulfillment, and inner peace.

Mary Allen, MCC
Author of *The Power of Inner Choice*

Elizabeth Barbour has elevated, simplified, and personalized the art of ritual and celebration in her new book *Sacred Celebrations: Designing Rituals to Navigate Life's Transitions*.

Whether you like to go all out, are a minimalist, or somewhere in between (the book has a handy guide for making this discernment), you will find not only practical advice and tips on creating rituals and celebrations for all kinds of milestones (some of which we typically don't mark or remember), but creative, moving, and meaningful examples from her own life and the lives of her friends and clients.

Sure, we've all celebrated birthdays and anniversaries, but there are many other life transitions that deserve presence, remembrance, or closure. Let *Sacred Celebrations* be your muse... you might be surprised at what you're wanting or willing to celebrate: from small daily moments to seasonal rituals to once-in-a-lifetime occurrences.

Karen C.L. Anderson, MCC
Author of *Difficult Mothers, Adult Daughters:*
A Guide For Separation, Liberation & Inspiration

Sacred Celebrations supports my work perfectly as a trauma-based therapist. Rituals bring light to what is deep down inside that needs healing. They give us simple yet powerful ways to move through life's challenges with a connection to something greater than ourselves. Elizabeth teaches that embracing the sacredness of life is where the energy of lasting transformation truly lives. I recommend this book for any coach, counselor, or healer that wants to take their work to a deeper level with their clients.

Dr. Shannon South
Award winning therapist, international trainer, and bestselling author of *Grow Your Business by Growing You: The Spiritual Entrepreneurs Guide to Maximum Joy, Abundance and Success*

This is a special book that everyone needs. It's a powerful tool for bringing closure. This is not just about celebration. It's really about endings and beginnings. It's about properly bringing closure to things and welcoming new opportunities and beginnings with intention. As someone who often needs to be prompted to celebrate, I find this book refreshing, insightful, and indispensable.

Lis Anna-Langston
Award winning author of *Tupelo Honey* and *Gobbledy*

In her book, Elizabeth Barbour taps into our soul's yearning for rituals amidst life's highs and lows. Merging relatable stories with keen insights, she unravels the dance between rituals, cherished traditions, and the ceremonies that dot our calendars. It's not just a book—it's a heartfelt guide urging you to treasure every fleeting moment.

Eva Gregory
author of *The Feel Good Guide To Prosperity*
and founder of the Enlightened Business Success Academy

I've read countless books on creating rituals and deepening our spiritual connections, but Elizabeth Barbour's *Sacred Celebrations* stands out as a beacon of truth and inspiration. It's a call to remember that we are all divine creatures and a guide to creating the rituals that help us honor and embody that divinity.

Dr. Sarah Long
Associate Professor of Rhetoric & Technical Writing
Appalachian State University
author of *Woman at the Devil's Door: The Untold True Story of the Hampsted Murderess*

What a transformational book! As a minister and spiritual life coach, I highly recommend Elizabeth Barbour's newest book which inspires and delights the reader. Whether you are an experienced sacred ritualist/ceremony leader or are new to the concept, you will love the way Elizabeth shares story after story about how ceremony and sacred ritual transform loss and the mundane into empowered and magical living. *Sacred Celebrations* encourages and inspires the practical use of ceremony in everyday life which is sure to help you experience greater joy, fulfillment, and peace—especially important in these times of uncertainty. Be sure to get your copy today!

Rev. Diana Kennedy
Development and Engagement Coordinator
Unity Worldwide Ministries

Reading Elizabeth Barbour's new book, *Sacred Celebrations: Designing Rituals to Navigate Life's Milestone Transitions* was a deeply moving experience. It gave me an opportunity to reflect on my entire life to date and see where ritual was successful and where a ritual would have been useful.

As I read each chapter, ideas began popping for improving my own daily, weekly, and monthly rituals, implementing more exciting and memorable ways to celebrate special occasions with family and friends and more cohesive ways to conduct rituals for my clients—in one-to-one work, group meetings, and retreats.

Elizabeth's goal to help us bring more joy and gratitude into our lives through sacred celebration can be achieved by allowing this beautiful book to be a reference guide, source of inspiration, and a deep unraveling of what no longer serves you so you can acknowledge the value of your life transitions and the life transitions of those you love and care for.

Baeth Davis
A Mentor to Mentors at YourPurpose.com

In a world so often too loud with the clamor of duty and responsibility-the risk is that we get so busy we miss our life!

Elizabeth Barbour has provided an inspiring guidebook for the modern woman to navigate change and connect more deeply to what matters most. With her unique life experience and compassionate heart, Elizabeth is uniquely qualified to author this work which sheds new light on established traditions and novel ways to celebrate the profound in our daily lives.

Sacred Celebrations is a beautiful gift for those at the multiple thresholds of change, growth, and loss that characterize a well-lived life.

Bev Martin
Intuition coach and life navigator

Sacred Celebrations

DESIGNING RITUALS TO NAVIGATE
LIFE'S MILESTONE TRANSITIONS

ELIZABETH BARBOUR

Copyright © 2023 by Elizabeth Barbour

Sacred Celebrations
Designing Rituals to Navigate Life's Milestone Transitions

All rights reserved.
No part of this work may be used or reproduced, transmitted, stored, or used in any form or by any means graphic, electronic, or mechanical, including but not limited to photocopying, recording, scanning, digitizing, taping, Web distribution, information networks or information storage and retrieval systems, or in any manner whatsoever without prior written permission from the publisher.

Senior Editor: Laurie Knight
Cover by: Kristina Edstrom

An Imprint for GracePoint Publishing (www.GracePointPublishing.com)

GracePoint Matrix, LLC
624 S. Cascade Ave, Suite 201
Colorado Springs, CO 80903
www.GracePointMatrix.com
Email: Admin@GracePointMatrix.com

SAN # 991-6032

Library of Congress Control Number: 2023949151

ISBN: (Paperback) 978-0-9724686-9-5
eISBN: 978-0-9893336-0-3

Books may be purchased for educational, business, or sales promotional use. For bulk order requests and price schedule contact:
Orders@GracePointPublishing.com

Dedication

To my sweet Riley Roo, the light of my life.

You show me daily what living a life of Sacred Celebration is all about.

Never stop being your sparkly, magical self!

Contents

Foreword iii
Preface vii
Part One Rituals and Why We Need Them 1
   Chapter One Honoring Cycles, Beginnings, and Endings 3
   Chapter Two A Little About Language 7
   Chapter Three What's Your Celebration Style? 13
   Chapter Four The True Power of Connection 19
   Chapter Five The Benefits of Celebration and Why We Resist It
.... 23
Part Two Life's Milestone Transitions 29
   Chapter Six Welcoming New Life 31
   Chapter Seven Birthdays 47
   Chapter Eight Growing Up 61
   Chapter Nine Weddings 71
   Chapter Ten Moving 81
   Chapter Eleven Divorce 93
   Chapter Twelve Death and Loss 107
   Chapter Thirteen Women's Transitions 125

Chapter Fourteen Health 139
Chapter Fifteen Business and Career 153
Part Three Rituals for Daily Living 163
Chapter Sixteen Morning Rituals 165
Chapter Seventeen Everyday Gratitude Rituals 171
Chapter Eighteen Family Rituals 179
Chapter Nineteen Develop Your Own Prayer Rituals 183
Chapter Twenty Home Altars 189
Chapter Twenty-One Holidays 195
Chapter Twenty-Two Cycles of Nature 201
Conclusion The World Needs More Rituals 207
Let's Stay Connected! 211
Acknowledgments 213
Notes 217
Resources 223
Elizabeth Barbour 225

Foreword

Elizabeth had already been a professional life and business coach for nearly two decades when we first met. She told me she had a book to write. She was also ready to incorporate her intuitive gifts and her training as a shamanic practitioner into her coaching practice. As she sat before me, she glowed with an *undeniable vibrancy* despite the many challenging events she had already encountered in her life. She had endured the pain of divorce, the death of both her parents, and the indescribable heartache of infertility. But she also knew the pure joy of becoming a parent through adoption, the thrill of growing a thriving business, and the adventure of moving multiple times to new cities. She explained that she had designed rituals to help navigate each of these milestone events in her life, and her enthusiasm and passion for this topic was potent!

She told me about her vision to help people everywhere learn how to access *ritual*. She grew animated as she discussed the simple yet profound ways that ritual had impacted her life and the lives of her coaching clients. As we began our work together, I realized that Elizabeth was standing on the threshold of stepping more fully into her life's purpose. I understood where she was because I was in a similar place when I'd decided to leave my medical practice to step onto the path of shamanism.

As I stood on that threshold between my old career and the unknown, a wise woman suggested that I do a fire ceremony. Knowing next to nothing about rituals, but trusting my intuition, I built a fire in our backyard fire pit with my husband's support. Using an empty Triscuit box, I tied old icky emails I had printed, my ID badge from the hospital, and a few other things onto it with string, creating a funky effigy of my medical career.

Once the fire was blazing, I called upon the spirit of the fire to help me. Then, I held my Triscuit box on my lap and thought about all the incredible gifts and lessons my career in medicine had given me. I also recalled all the things about that work that I was ready to leave behind. When I felt complete, I set the box into the fire and let it go. I'll never forget when the fire dramatically leaped up and my effigy-cracker box blossomed into the ashy shape of my favorite flower, a peony. At that moment, I knew that everything was going to work out and soon after, I was able to gracefully exit medicine.

When we signal to the spiritual realms that we are ready for a change through performing a ritual, it causes shifts to happen in this ordinary world.

Life's unexpected plot twists aren't up to us. And as Elizabeth so warmly shares in this empowering book: "It is ritual that can help make these transitions feel more meaningful, joyful, and manageable." We understand, through ritual, that we are never alone on this wacky and "brutiful" (as Glennon Doyle refers to it, beautiful plus brutal) path we call life.

In *Sacred Celebrations*, Elizabeth covers the gamut of Big. Life. Changes. She teaches us how to celebrate the highs and honor the lows. Whether performed alone or in a group, we are fortified and purified by rituals that allow us to step into a sacred space. We are all walking, talking altars. We are here to support each other with kindness through the magic and mystery of this earthly life. *We were born knowing how to do these things.*

Foreword

Elizabeth will show you how to be fully present in the midst of the chaos and make sense of the swirling emotions of whatever life event you're experiencing. When you read this book, you will feel emboldened and empowered to create a one-of-a-kind ritual for yourself or someone you love, and that ritual will change the world in the best way!

As is evidenced in this book, you don't have to be a shaman, priest, or professional celebrant, you just need to bring your heart.

I am grateful she has written this book. You will be too. Take time to savor it, read it slowly, or simply open it up to the chapter that pertains to you at this time. Be sure to read the chapters about daily rituals that you can incorporate into your life to make it more enchanting and meaningful. You'll want to keep this book in your library as a reference for all the celebrations and for all the hard things too. You'll want to give it to young people who are just beginning their adult lives with so many beautiful and powerful rituals ahead of them.

Let this book inspire the ritual that you need in *this moment* of your life.

I have a hunch that honoring yourself (or another being) in this way will lead to some powerful magic.

With gratitude,
Sarah Bamford Seidelmann

Sarah Bamford Seidelmann, MD, is a fourth-generation physician, a shamanic healer, and a Master Coach and instructor trained at the Martha Beck Institute. She is the author of six books, including The Book of Beasties *(about the wisdom of spirit animals),* Swimming with Elephants *(her hilarious and poignant memoir about her spiritual awakening) and* Where the Deer Dream *(a coming-of-age adventure in spirit book). Sarah believes it is self-expression that creates health and vitality in human beings and encourages everybody she meets to* make things *(songs, plays, paintings, salads, flower arrangements, sacred ceremonies, and art).*

Preface

My mom died in the humid late summer Texas heat on the evening of September 11, 2016. I was with her when she took her last breath. It was just the two of us alone—my daughter's pink teddy bear curled up under her arm and Beethoven playing softly in the background in her tranquil room at the stately brick mansion that hosts the Houston Hospice House. I held her hand and thanked her for being the best mom she knew how to be, and I told her how grateful I was that she was finally at peace because she had suffered so much in her final years.

We had a complicated relationship. For twenty-five years, we never lived in the same city. As soon as I graduated from high school I got as far away from home as I could, and it wasn't until she was diagnosed with stage IV lung cancer in January 2013 that she moved to Houston, Texas so that I could help care for her.

During the three-and-a-half years we battled her cancer together, we had an opportunity to make our peace. I got to know the *real* her without the cloud of alcohol that had consumed most of her life. Joan was surprisingly funny. She was also stubborn, fiercely independent, and determined. At only 4'11" and seventy-two pounds by the time she died, she was a teeny tiny package made of steel.

Our relationship was complex. Others saw my mom's *best* self—her impeccable manners, her outgoing personality, and her *volunteer* self who was incredibly generous. But I, along with a few close relatives, got the brunt of her critical, controlling, overbearing, narcissistic ways. She had a tortured childhood, a less-than-ideal marriage with my dad, and she never believed in therapy or asking for help. As a result, she drank to survive.

But I loved her, too. She taught me to appreciate a well-written novel, classical music, and the joy of volunteering time and talents. She played a mean game of Scrabble, was "the hostess with the mostess," and valued education (mine) above all else. She devoted her life to making sure that I was loved and cared for in a way she never experienced.

As she was fighting for her life, I had a front-row seat to her courage, bravery, and sheer fortitude. My daughter was only two at the time of Mom's diagnosis and Mom had waited *so long* to be a grandma. Riley was her inspiration, her *raison d'être*, and we shared many sweet moments of our three generations during those twilight years. We all knew Mom was simply buying herself some time with the grueling cancer treatments, but it was quality time. Not only did she earn precious moments with her beloved granddaughter, but we also got a chance to heal and forgive our decades-long rift.

A feisty, proud Connecticut Yankee, she had retired to Clearwater, Florida, and lived there for almost twenty years after the death of my father in 1994. She had a supportive circle of friends, actively volunteered, and lived near her beloved sister and my cousins.

I remember when she came to the difficult decision to sell her home in Florida and relocate to Houston, her dyed-in-the-wool East Coast self said, "You mean, I'm really going to die in Texas?"

A few months before the cancer came back, I asked her what types of music and readings she might like at her memorial service, and she said, "I don't even want one."

I retorted, "Well, it's not for you because you'll be gone. It's for me and others who want to remember you."

"If it's for you, then you plan it. You don't need my help!" she replied indignantly.

So, I did. She didn't want anything, yet she got *two* celebrations of her life.

Five days after Mom made her transition, I hosted a white rose release ceremony at my home. My intention was only to host one formal funeral for her in Florida, but my friend Danielle insisted that my Houston friends wanted to show their support, and she urged me to plan a gathering. So, I hastily made some quick decisions, and I invited my female friends to help me honor my mother—and their mothers—with a simple ceremony of walking to the creek and releasing white roses together. I intentionally held this gathering in the morning when I knew my husband would be at work and my daughter would be in kindergarten. I needed to be surrounded by feminine energy in my first official goodbye to the woman who had nurtured me for most of my life.

Why white roses? White roses are symbolic of eternal love and are sometimes called "flowers of light." We come from the light, and we return to the light. They also represent unchanging loyalty and symbolize that love is stronger than death.

The morning of the gathering, I lay in the fetal position in bed, unable to move. We have access to ministers and rabbis and other holy people to help facilitate funerals because it allows space and time for the family to grieve and feel all their emotions. But for some crazy reason, I had decided that Mom's first send-off should be fully planned and executed by me, her only child. What was I thinking?

Slowly, my circle started gathering and my jangled nerves calmed down with each hug I received. More than thirty women arrived from all aspects of my life in Houston, neighbors, church friends, book club members, networking colleagues, clients, and Zumba dance buddies—only three or four had actually met my mother. They all gathered *for me*. This diverse group of women all enjoyed meeting one another, and my home and my heart overflowed with the rich sounds of women talking and laughing together.

I gathered the guests in the living room and stood on the staircase of the high-ceilinged great room so I could drink in the lovely faces and bask in their supportive energy. I thanked everyone for coming and invited each woman to take a white rose from the basket and slowly walk down the meandering trail to the bridge. I encouraged them to make new friends and to talk intentionally about their mothers—share good memories, a funny story, maybe a favorite food they made, or challenges they might have or have had with their mothers. I wanted this day to not be just about my mother, but about all the mothers in our lives.

I was the last one out of the house and walked at the back of the group that snaked along the gravel pathway, watching the women talking with heads bowed in groups of twos and threes. One friend brought my sweet black lab mix, Daisy, on a leash—her wagging tail, a bright spot for all of us.

Under the hot sun, we gathered in a semi-circle at the bridge, and with a deep breath, I plunged into sharing my mom's life story. I told them about her difficult childhood growing up in an orphanage after the Great Depression and about the unthinkable abuse she endured. I described how, on her eighteenth birthday, she packed her bags, walked down the street and rented a room at the YWCA because she knew in her bones that a whole world was out there waiting for her, and she was going to go find it. I shared the story of how she met my dad (he lived across the street from her when she was unofficially adopted in her twenties by the people who I knew as my grandparents) and about my seemingly idyllic childhood growing up in Connecticut. But I also told them about her raging alcoholism and how it impacted those closest to her. I recounted her later years and her decade of hospice volunteer work, about her being a proud P.E.O. (Philanthropic Education Organization) sister, and about her brave three-and-a-half-year battle with cancer. I told them how, even though it had been very challenging between us for decades, in the final years of her life, we were able to have great healing and forgiveness.

We were all sweating profusely under the cloudless Texas sky, but my women friends held me during this sacred time. They listened. They witnessed as my mom's story and my story comingled. They beamed love to hold me up in a time of deep grief.

I remember at one point looking around the semi-circle and feeling the love being shown to me. A few women carried umbrellas to shade themselves from the sun, but all held their white roses and gave me their undivided attention and love. Daisy was the only one brave enough to wade into the creek below to cool off her belly, providing us with a wonderful spot of comic relief in the oppressive heat of the day.

When I stopped recounting Joan's life, I knew I wanted them to connect with their own mother figures—moms, grandmothers, aunties, and more. I invited everyone present to speak aloud the names of their mothers in unison. You could hear a collective mumble of "Susan. Betty. Virginia. Adele. Sandra. Rosemary," as the women quietly shared the names as though praying aloud in church.

Then my group facilitator training kicked into gear, and I invited them to go around the space and share a word or phrase that was a gift they received from their mothers. At first, there were murmurs and then their voices lifted strong and clear. "Love. Laughter. Strength. Tenacity. Love of cooking. Wisdom. Tenderness. The importance of family."

It was a powerful moment together reflecting on the benefits we receive from the mother figures in our lives. The energy had shifted from me as the focal point of the conversation to a collective remembrance of our mothers, living or dead. It was the perfect time to pivot and honor them all—their memories and stories, joys, and sacrifices.

I explained the significance of the white roses and described the three grief rituals I had done to help prepare Mom for her transition. Then we all lined up at the edge of the faded wooden bridge, and on the count of three, we lovingly and intentionally released our roses into the water below.

For a few minutes, we stood there mesmerized, leaning over the edge of the wooden railing to gaze at the flowers. The water was a dark bluish-brown and the white blooms created a beautiful pattern as they scattered in the water.

After the ceremony, we meandered back down the pathway, and everyone commented on how gorgeous our scenery was with the flowing creek, green grass, blue sky, white puffy clouds.

One friend cast a glance backward and noticed that the roses had crossed underneath the bridge. We remarked on how symbolic the movement paralleled my mom's transition across the veil from her earthly body to her heavenly one.

Some traditions believe it takes the soul several days to leave the body. It was as though Mom was sending a message saying, "I made it!"

We came back to my house and ate all of Mom's favorite foods: watermelon, ice cream, Starbucks Frappuccinos, and even chardonnay before lunch! Everyone remarked what an amazing person she was to have survived so much, and they were grateful that I had shared her personal stories with them.

When everyone left, I fell into a deep slumber for several hours, and when I woke up, I was calm and peaceful. Despite the struggles that we had in our relationship, I loved my mother and had great respect for her strength and resilience. I knew that she loved me fiercely and it was incredibly sad to accept that my biggest champion and cheerleader was gone. Being able to do a life review and share her stories through laughter and tears while being witnessed by my women friends was powerful medicine on my healing journey.

Creating the white rose ceremony and intentionally asking my community for support gave me the container to process the early stages of both my grief and my relief. It allowed me to gain clarity, get grounded, feel more balanced, and really receive the emotional support I needed. I knew the formal funeral in Florida lay ahead but I needed something less formal and more intimate, as balm. The white rose ceremony was a critical step for me to begin the honoring and celebration of her just a few days after she died while I was still in a place of deep grief.

Part One
Rituals and Why We Need Them

Celebration and ritual have long been a key component of my work and my life before I truly understood what they were—*a sacred container for transformation and healing*. Over the years, I have created dozens of my own personal rituals, and I have coached clients and supported friends in all sorts of celebrations. Some of these were traditional gatherings like birthdays, anniversaries, retirements, weddings, baby showers, and funerals, but with a more personally tailored spin. Others were less common, but equally important rituals of grief like honoring a divorce or recognizing job loss. And still other rituals of invention or reinvention aid in transitions like a new home purchase, starting a business, changing careers, or honoring the transition to becoming empty nesters. It is, without a doubt, some of the most important work I was put on the planet to do.

Perhaps you have a joyful event coming up in your life and you want to plan it with meaning. Or you have recently had a significant loss and you want to honor it in a way that is purposeful, meaningful, and filled with love and intention. Maybe you have had the privilege of attending a gathering that was so profound and moving that you want *your* next celebration to have that WOW factor or transcendent experience that leaves people feeling nurtured and inspired.

Change is hard. Whether it is good or bad, change involves uncertainty and can bring out our greatest fears. Having a baby is simultaneously joyful and terrifying. Moving is similarly exhilarating and a step into the unknown. Starting a new business is freeing and overwhelming.

Creating containers to honor those significant changes can help us navigate uncertain waters with more clarity and confidence. If you crave a deeper connection to self, community, and source, I look forward to exploring this with you. It is my deepest desire to support you in living a life of delightful wholeness, and that starts with adding more celebration!

Chapter One
Honoring Cycles, Beginnings, and Endings

Throughout my career as a coach, I have guided my clients through the many cycles of life. Call them stages, seasons, or chapters. No matter what word resonates, life is filled with them.

Whether we are talking about the monthly cycles of the moon, a woman's menstruation, the academic year calendar, the four seasons of Mother Nature, the life cycle of a butterfly, the flow of oxygen and carbon dioxide in the atmosphere, or the cycles of the stock market, we live in a world that has cycles and rhythms.

Beginnings are the starting points. They are the first part, early period, or origin point of any new venture. Beginnings are exciting for some because they are fresh, new, and open to possibilities. Others dread starting something new because they prefer comfort, familiarity, and maintaining the status quo. Some beginnings are by choice and others are forced whether you like them or not.

Having support—an encouraging best friend, a supportive neighbor, or an inspiring business coach—along the way is critical. That is why schools offer new student orientation, churches offer premarital counseling, and corporations have onboarding programs. Whether starting a new year, a new business, or a new relationship, the more intentionally and mindfully you can engage in the process, the more likely you are to be successful.

It's important to begin things properly by gathering information, having clear communication, setting expectations, and being aware of any potential pitfalls. When an architect designs a new house, they don't sit down and start drawing right away. They take time to visit the land, interview the client to understand their big vision and values, and how they want to interact in the space. Then the architect takes time to sketch out ideas on paper and present it to their client.

Consider a couple that meets, falls in love, and decides to marry quickly. Chances are good that the couple may not last as long as a couple who spends a year or two getting to know each other before deciding to tie the knot. As a good friend of mine says, "You should go through all four seasons with a significant other before deciding to marry. Someone might be playful and fun in the summertime but have major conflict with their family over the holidays. You want to experience all of that before committing for the long term." Of course, there are always exceptions.

The completion of a cycle might look like the end of the day, a week, the school year, a big work project, or having kids at home.

Just like with the conclusion or summary of a research paper, it is important to wrap things up with a pretty bow. When you are completing a job, moving out of a home, or ending a relationship, it is important to end that cycle with integrity, good communication, and gratitude, wrapping up any loose ends to feel complete.

That is why so many people who may have previously been estranged make an effort to reconcile and make peace when a loved one is dying.

When sending a child off to college, it is essential for the family to cherish and celebrate their final weeks or months at home, knowing that this chapter of life is coming to an end.

Retirement can also bring up a lot of emotions for people, especially for someone who has identified with their work for so long. It is important to honor, recognize, and celebrate accomplishments, relationships, impact, and legacy before sending them on their way into the next chapter as a retiree.

Chapter Two
A Little About Language

Ritual, celebrations, and traditions have the transformative power to help people navigate life's biggest changes. Let us begin by discussing the distinctions between some key words that we will be using in this book.

Sacred refers to anything that helps a person transcend the mundane and feel connected to the Divine, the spiritual world, God, or a higher power. Something worthy of awe and respect—whether it is a person, place, object, or experience—can be considered sacred. It does not need to be religious in nature, but it certainly can be. Prayer time, a spiritual talisman, a magical place in the forest, or a meaningful gathering of friends are all sacred.

Celebrations are occasions where people gather to express their happiness and joy over a particular event. They are often planned affairs where friends, family, and colleagues gather to share their good tidings with one another. Birthdays, weddings, graduation parties, and baby showers are all traditional examples of celebrations, but life gives us other important occasions to celebrate including a first tooth, earning a driver's license, accepting a new job, and starting a business.

A **ceremony** is an event of ritual significance, usually performed on a special occasion. It comes from the Latin root *caerimoniae*, to mean "ritual prescriptions" or "ritual acts." For example, a wedding celebration may last for hours or days with the religious ceremony itself, the wedding, the pivotal part.

The word *ritual* comes from the Latin root word *ritus* which means "rite" and can refer to either a religious ceremony or social custom. Rituals are often ceremonial in nature. They include specific actions and intentions to support an outcome. We can think of rituals in a variety of ways—as stemming from religious traditions or as something done regularly so that it becomes a habit (i.e., drinking coffee is a morning ritual).

Traditions are customs, often inherited from previous generations, or from an entire culture, that people expect to do repeatedly over time. Recognizing holidays every year often involves traditions. They can be handed down from ancestors and passed forward to children of the next generation. Eating black-eyed peas for good luck on New Year's, making Grandma's pumpkin pie recipe at Thanksgiving, or going to the same restaurant on the anniversary of a first date are all great examples.

Consider a wedding, for example.

A wedding celebration may extend for a few days including a bachelor/bachelorette party, the rehearsal dinner, the wedding itself, and a brunch the morning after the wedding. The entire sequence of events is all part of the celebration of the union of two people. In some traditions, this may take a day or a weekend, in others it may be a week-long affair.

Chapter Two: A Little About Language

Mary Allen and John Cole traveled from the US to India with their elementary school-age twins to attend the wedding of the daughter of one of John's business colleagues. It was a five-day affair that involved lavish parties, delicious food, high profile guests, and required several changes of clothing! Mary described it as a once-in-a-lifetime opportunity to experience a Hindu wedding and to expose her children to cultural traditions different from her own.

The wedding ceremony is where two people actually become married legally and spiritually, so it is perhaps the most important part of the bigger celebration. The ceremony may only be fifteen minutes in a simple wedding, or perhaps an hour-long mass as in a Catholic wedding. The ceremony is facilitated by a clergy person such as a priest, minister, or rabbi but can also be conducted by a justice of the peace, celebrant, or a notary public.

Key elements in a ceremony include the processional, invocation, declaration of intent, vows, ring exchange, and pronouncement. Additional enhancements may include readings, music, and other rituals specific to the couple and their family customs. My friends Shonnie Lavender and Bruce Mulkey wrote a book called I Do! I Do! The Marriage Vow Workbook, and it's a wonderful resource for anyone wanting to write heartfelt and meaningful vows to their beloved.

Wedding rituals are usually embedded into the wedding ceremony and can be deeply symbolic. They may include the exchange of rings, saying vows to one another, unity rituals (burning a unity candle, mixing sand together, etc.), the breaking of the glass at a Jewish wedding, and hand fasting (a pagan ritual at the end of the ceremony as the final promise to bind their lives together).

When Rev. Shad married his wife, instead of a traditional ring bearer, they opted to have their wedding rings passed around on a silk pillow and be blessed by the friends and family in attendance. Their rings were passed up and down the rows and people were invited to hold the rings and infuse them with their love and blessings for the couple before they placed them on their fingers.

Wedding traditions often include elements like the bride carrying a bouquet of flowers, a wedding cake, or something old, something new, something borrowed, something blue.

When Eric and I got married, we opted to eschew the traditional wedding cake and instead serve blackberry cobbler, a family favorite. His Aunt Martha painstakingly handpicked ten gallons of blackberries from the family farm in Eastern North Carolina. We used his grandmother's recipe. As a wedding gift, I commissioned my very talented friend Mista Whitson to paint Eric's family farm of which he is the fifth-generation owner. I arranged for it to be revealed on the "cake table" (more accurately, the cobbler table) so when we went over to cut the cobbler, I surprised Eric with this gift. I took the opportunity to grab the microphone and explained to our guests the significance of the painting and the delicious cobbler!

Throughout the book, some of these terms may be used interchangeably but know that the theme that ties them all together is the sacredness of connecting with intention. Language is powerful and how you choose to use or interpret a word is what matters the most. While it's important to be as inclusive as possible when planning an event, don't worry too much about getting caught up on finding the perfect words to describe your gathering. Focus on the overall emotional experience that you want to create for yourself and your guests.

Chapter Three
What's Your Celebration Style?

While writing this book, I talked with a lot of people about celebration. Because it is a core value, I initially assumed that everybody would appreciate it and approach it the same way I did.

Boy, was I wrong!

There are many factors that influence how someone approaches celebration. Were you raised in a household that recognized celebrations at all? Did you get gifts or parties as a child? If you had parties, were they simple or lavish? In some families, simply baking cupcakes or treating the birthday person to a favorite meal is considered a family party. In other families, throwing big gatherings with lots of guests and hiring professional entertainment (like face painting clowns for the kids and live musicians for the adults) may be the norm.

Or did your family downplay special occasions or bypass them altogether?

What were the beliefs in your home about celebrations? Some more expressive families find them as a way to communicate love, build connections, and honor other family members. Other more reserved families may feel grand celebrations are excessive, too emotional, or draw too much attention to one particular person or event.

Over time, I've arrived at the unscientific conclusion that there are three main types of styles of people who celebrate: the enthusiast, the traditionalist, and the minimalist. I think even the avoiders, with some coaxing and encouragement, might really be minimalists at heart. *Ha ha!*

Perhaps you have never even considered your celebration style. As you go through this book, I encourage you to be intentional about the types of rituals and celebrations that you want to embrace.

Take this short quiz to discover your celebration style.

What's Your Celebration Style?

1. When you celebrate your birthday do you prefer to…
    A. Go out and party with a big group of friends?
    B. Have a small family dinner?
    C. Celebrate by yourself or with just one other person?
2. When you find out that a friend got engaged, what do you do next?
    A. Start planning their engagement party, thinking about all the special ways to honor and recognize the union of friends.
    B. Ask them about their family traditions and plans for their wedding.
    C. Send a card.
3. When you're moving away from a city or neighborhood, how do you say goodbye to your friends?
    A. Throw a big party and invite everyone. It's important to say final goodbyes and feel closure on this chapter of life!

Chapter Three: What's Your Celebration Style?

   B. Plan a small cookout in my backyard with my closest neighbors.
   C. Sneak out of town quietly and don't look back.
4. When planning your wedding or helping someone you love to plan theirs, which idea do you absolutely adore?
   A. Engage someone to compose original music for my ceremony.
   B. Read a traditional poem or religious text that parents or grandparents included in their wedding.
   C. Keep vows simple and straightforward. No muss, no fuss.
5. What's your preferred environment for a big celebration?
   A. A large and lavish event venue.
   B. My grandmother's backyard or on our family land.
   C. Someplace out in nature, the woods, or by the ocean.
6. When planning a party, what do you think about finances?
   A. The sky is the limit. Only the best for a party!
   B. It is important to create a budget for optimal planning.
   C. I have no desire to spend a lot of money. It's the intention and meaning of the gathering that matters most, so just the essentials.
7. When you celebrate Thanksgiving with your family, what are you most likely to prepare?
   A. Plan it for weeks ahead of time with dozens of dishes.
   B. Use all of our family recipes, year after year.
   C. Order takeout sushi, tacos, or pizza.
8. You are planning your sister's baby shower. What does it look like?
   A. Filled with great ideas (thanks Pinterest!) to plan for fancy foods, fun games, and playful decorations.

- B. Call our mom/grandmother/sister and find out what other baby showers in our family have looked like over the years.
- C. Take her out to lunch with a few inner circle friends and family.
9. You find out your best friend is getting divorced. What do you do to show your support and solidarity?
    - A. Help her create a divorce party or a ritual with friends so she can honor the grief of her loss but also the possibilities for her future.
    - B. Send her flowers and a heartfelt note.
    - C. Call and text her regularly, checking in to make sure she's doing okay.
10. You've recently learned about the death of your close friend's parent. What do you do?
    - A. Deliver a care package of self-care goodies and a book about grief.
    - B. Send flowers and attend the funeral.
    - C. Send a card and give her a phone call in a few weeks after all the hubbub has died down.

If most of your answers were A, then you're likely to be an enthusiast.

If most of your answers were B, then you're likely to be a traditionalist.

If most of your answers were C, then you're likely to be a minimalist.

The Enthusiast—A person preferring this celebration style embraces life's events with passion and zeal. They appreciate the value of a good party or a meaningful ceremony. They enjoy introducing people to one another to create friendships and build community. They may be more emotional and see the value in expressing their range of emotions from joy to grief as a way of processing the world around them.

Some Qualities of the Enthusiast:
- Celebrates all the meaningful details.
- Reveres life's defining moments.
- Deeply honors change and transition.
- Enjoys engaging in the sensory elements.
- Loves bringing people together in the name of celebration.

The Traditionalist—The individual with this celebration style may have a strong sense of connection to family and previous generations. Perhaps they were raised in a household that regularly honored their ancestors. Or, if they didn't grow up in that environment, they desire that and are consciously infusing their current family situation with time-honored traditions.

Some Qualities of the Traditionalist:
- Honors and respects tradition that is already in place.
- Embraces "This is how we've always done it" but may add a personal twist or modern flair.
- Collects letters or photographs about family ancestry; acts as family historian.
- Asks family members for their recollections of special occasions with parents and grandparents.
- Cherishes memories from childhood and wants to recreate those for their own children.

The Minimalist—The person with this celebration style tends to be low-key. They value change and transition and understand the importance of honoring it, but don't feel the need to be over-the-top with their expressions. They tend to value small gestures and understated expressions of appreciation.

Some Qualities of the Minimalist:
- Embraces the idea that less is more.
- Approaches events to keep them simple and streamlined.
- Leans toward smaller groups and gatherings.
- Values repurposing and recycling as good for Mother Earth.
- Seems grounded and simple in approaches (Zen, hippie, earthy).

This isn't a perfect science, and you might find yourself between two styles. Be sure to embrace whichever style you feel drawn to at the moment. Yearly birthdays might be small affairs with your closest family members but when you decide to get married, it may be a more elaborate occasion.

Now that you have a sense of your style, as you go through the book and read about these rituals and traditions, remember that you can tailor each suggestion according to your style. It doesn't matter what your personal style or preference is. What matters is that you approach the art and science of creating a ritual with attention and intention. Whether it's a simple daily act like adorning yourself with beautiful jewelry or planning a once in a lifetime affair like retiring after a successful career, the key is to get creative and have fun with this!

Chapter Four
The True Power of Connection

I've moved a lot. I've lived in thirteen cities in eight states in the past thirty years. I've lived in North Carolina four separate times in four different cities. I consider the mountains of Asheville my "heart home" and at the same time I still identify as being a Connecticut Yankee since that's where I was raised.

Much like military families who are constantly relocating, I've learned to adapt well to change, and I've gotten good at making new friends everywhere I go. Since becoming a business owner in 2000, I've lived in four different states, so to keep my business flourishing, I must dive right into a new community and extend myself.

Flashback to 2002: I was sitting on the back deck of my condo that overlooked downtown Asheville, North Carolina, with two friends and colleagues having an informal mastermind chat. Ginger was an established graphic designer and Totsie was a talented website designer, and I was in the early days of growing my coaching business. I had invited them to my house so that we could brainstorm ideas for each of our businesses to discuss the challenges we were facing, identify the opportunities, and put our heads together to see how we could solve problems and create solutions.

As I was talking about my marketing efforts and business services, one of them said, "You need to teach other people how to network because you do it so well."

I scoffed and said, "Surely nobody would pay me for that. Everyone knows how to network. Don't they?"

They both quickly responded, "Absolutely not! Networking is an art and a skill. You connect with people so effortlessly, but it doesn't come naturally for many of us."

They encouraged me to start teaching workshops on how to network and when I implemented those, I didn't spend money on marketing or advertising for many years because I developed a huge community through my networking events and, as a result, business naturally flowed my way.

I've heard these statements repeatedly in my life:

"Gosh, you have *so* many friends!"

"You sure are extroverted! Where do you get your energy from?"

"You throw really good parties!"

"I always meet interesting people thanks to you."

"You sure know how to celebrate!"

It has often been said that many of the gifts and talents we develop as adults come from wounds we experienced in our childhood. I was placed for adoption at birth and grew up knowing I was adopted. My parents always made me feel special and loved, but I knew that I was different from my friends. The core trauma of adoption stems from the primal wound of an infant being separated from its biological mother at birth, and it manifests as a fear of abandonment. So it makes sense that, as a child with the cellular memory of being separated from my biological mother, one of my core drives as a human being would be to create connections with people so that I could never be abandoned again.

Throughout my life, I have experienced being abandoned by boyfriends or girlfriends who decided they no longer wanted to be my friend, but I have always had a large group of friends to fall back on and help me through those rough spots. Even though I was hurt and grieving the loss of those relationships, I never truly felt alone.

According to *The Longevity Project,* a book about an eighty-year study of longevity, one of the top three factors in living a long life is having a supportive community of friends. Having a social network is even more important than diet, exercise, or the presence of an active religious life.[1]

The idea to write this book came to me when I was having a conversation with Hayley Foster, a coach who specializes in helping people with their short talks (think TED-style talks). I hired her for a one-hour consultation not knowing that it would become the turning point in my life as a writer. Our conversation made me realize that the book I had been laboring over for years was not the book I was *supposed* to be writing—it was this one.

She asked what I was passionate about, and I told her three things: gathering people in community, exploring my spiritual life, and designing and facilitating rituals.

The night before our phone call, I had been talking with a friend and after we hung up, I walked into my office and made a list of more than a dozen rituals that I had designed and experienced in my life. I don't know what prompted me to make the list but when I got on the phone with Hayley, I was ready to dive deep.

We discussed how disconnected people have become—from themselves, from others, and from a Higher Power—and that what they are craving is connection, community, and spiritual guidance. During that short but pivotal conversation is when I realized not only do I love providing those things for others, but I also especially love teaching others how to create it for themselves.

A survey of about 10,000 people conducted in 2019 by Cigna using the UCLA Loneliness Scale showed that a whopping 61 percent of participants identified as feeling lonely. This number went up 7 percent from the previous year. [2]

A more recent report from Harvard's Making Caring Common Project taken during the pandemic in October 2020 showed that one in three survey respondents reported serious loneliness and that 61 percent of young adults (eighteen to twenty-five) and 51 percent of young mothers reported the same. This was a smaller sample of about 950 respondents.[3]

We are desperate for connection with one another because we want to be seen and heard. We value finding parallels with others because it helps us feel less alone and more understood. When advising my coaching clients who have expressed their loneliness and isolation during our work together, one of the first remedies I suggest is the ritual of building community. Join a book club. Take a yoga class. Start a supper club. Volunteer at a non-profit. Meet weekly for coffee with a trusted friend. Building a regular ritual will help to increase a sense of connection and improve overall health and well-being.

Chapter Five
The Benefits of Celebration and Why We Resist It

When we connect more deeply to ourselves and to others, we experience more moments of gratitude. When we slow down, we can be more fully present to the miracles of everyday living—the cardinal chirping on the windowsill, the uplifting song on the radio on the drive to work, the gurgling laughter of a grandbaby—and feel the joy in our hearts, even when times are tough.

Oprah Winfrey once said, "The more you celebrate your life, the more there is in your life to celebrate."[4]

I agree with Oprah. Celebration is good for us. Studies have shown that when we live our lives from a place of celebration and gratitude, we are happier, healthier, more resilient, less stressed, and we have a stronger sense of community.

In the business world, celebration provides motivation and inspiration to achieve goals and can be a great way to celebrate excellence in the workplace. Celebrations of goals or anniversaries with the company can offer examples to team members that inspire them to take action toward their own vision of success.

In the sports community, victories on the playing field are celebrated with great enthusiasm. They are also studied in detail to understand what contributed to the win and how to replicate that level of success in the future.

So, it follows that celebrating personal milestone events is equally as important as celebrating a workplace goal achieved or a win on the playing field. There are so many benefits of celebrating life's big transitions as well as the smaller wins. Consider the following:

Celebrations feel good. Celebrations trigger a dopamine release in our brains. And if it feels good, we want more of it. Celebrations often involve sensory elements that we enjoy on noteworthy occasions—specially prepared foods, delicious drinks, candlelight or fireworks, music that inspires us to dance. We also appreciate quality time spent with friends and family, especially if we don't see them on a regular basis. Who doesn't want more laughter, fun, and dancing in their lives, right?

Celebrations encourage us to connect with our community. Think about some of the most important celebrations in life—birthdays, weddings, anniversaries, job promotions, retirement, etc. These are all social gatherings to acknowledge the important milestones in our lives. When we share those big events with people who care about us, it can really amp up the joy. A birthday gathering with three people may be perfect for the minimalist but a birthday party with thirty may be just the way the enthusiast wants to celebrate!

Celebrations build self-esteem. Whether it's receiving an award at work or having friends throw a surprise birthday party, being the center of love and adoration builds confidence and is good for the mind, body, and spirit. The student who earns an award in front of the whole school for achieving a 4.0 GPA is likely to continue to be a strong student because of the positive message being reinforced by recognizing their hard work. The friend who just endured a terrible romantic breakup and is single again will be buoyed by friends who plan a birthday party with all her favorite things, reminding her of how well she is loved.

Rituals make occasions memorable. Whether it is a birthday marking the passage of time, a wedding to celebrate the union of two people, or a retirement party to acknowledge the end of a career, rituals help us to celebrate the significant milestones in our lives. When we look back at our lives, we tend to remember these special occasions. We remember where the gathering was held, what we wore, what the weather was, what funny jokes were told, and who stood out in the crowd.

Rituals create a container to connect with the Divine. The routine of our daily lives can be very mundane. We get up, send the kids off to school, go to work, come home and make dinner, do chores, maybe play a game or enjoy some family time, then we go to bed and do it all over again. But when we take time to pause—whether it's savoring a morning cup of tea, the act of lighting candles and saying grace at the dinner table or going to church or temple once a week—it helps us to connect to something greater than ourselves.

We are disconnected from spiritual life in our modern chaotic information age, and we need to consciously take time to reconnect with our spiritual practices. When we do this, we are able to transform our chaos to calm, flip from anxiety to flow, and shift from feeling tired to living inspired.

Rituals give us permission to feel deeply. Somewhere along the way in Western culture, we got the notion that we need to keep our feelings to ourselves. If we are too joyful, people might be jealous. If we are too sad, people might be uncomfortable. Keep it neutral to get through life okay. Well, that is not how we are wired!

Humans are designed with a wide range of emotions that we are capable of feeling on any given day and at any given moment. Rituals help us to process feelings and emotions that are too big for ordinary days.

Rituals ease transitions. Change can be hard, and it is helpful to have some time to mark the end of one chapter of our lives and the beginning of the next. The tradition of taking a honeymoon after a wedding allows the couple to have quality intimate time together as life partners, and revel in their newfound status as a married couple before returning to the real world. The Jewish tradition of sitting shiva for seven days after a loved one has died is another example. During this time, the immediate family receives visitors at their home, and they are able to openly express their grief over the loss of their beloved. Graduation parties are another good example of learning how to let go and say goodbye. Parents who are preparing to send their child off to college or to begin a new job need support just as much as the eighteen-year-old who is heading out into the world.

Rituals invite 100 percent presence. When fully conscious in the moment where internal noise and distractions fall away, there is the opportunity to fully experience one's environment with a heightened sense of presence. Try to recall a very special day, like a wedding or the birth of a child. While many experiences are recalled as a blur, there are also poignant moments etched fully in the brain because of the complete presence of all five senses. For example, the moment of vows being exchanged during a wedding may be more readily recalled than the fogginess of the people visiting during the reception. The recollection of exhausting struggles of labor softens over time, yet the first holding or suckling or cutting of the umbilical cord is still precise in its emotional imprint.

Rituals allow us to rest. Rest is healing—life-giving—and helps us to press the reset buttons on our lives. When experiencing a huge change, rest is the best way to manage it... to clear the calendar, delete the to-do list, and to say no to everything but the most essential things. Rest is critical for our mind, body, and spirit. Rituals provide us space and time to breathe, to be, and to rest.

What if You Don't Like to Celebrate?

Many people don't like to celebrate. It is almost as though there is an aversion to authentic celebration. Is it our Puritan roots? Believing that we don't deserve to be happy, experience joy, and celebrate life?

Sadly, there are too many of us who learn at a young age that we shouldn't be proud of our accomplishments, toot our own horn, or celebrate too extravagantly. The messages we hear include:

- You're too much/too loud.
- You're too big for your britches.
- You're selfish.
- Your ego is too big.

Or maybe it's the experiences we have had in our lives:

- Being let down (hoping for recognition but not getting it).
- Being overshadowed (by another sibling or parent who craved attention and edged you out).
- Being shamed (why do you need the spotlight?).

My mom was a perfect example. She grew up in an orphanage during the Depression. Money was scarce and affection for the children, scarcer still. Cupcakes for birthdays were almost non-existent. She learned to downplay any big events in her life because no one had taught her how to celebrate as a child.

My coaching client, Shonda, told me she was about to celebrate ten years in business. When I asked her how she planned to celebrate, she gazed at me with a blank stare. She said, "I guess I should do something… But what if nobody shows up?" She went on to reference a birthday party from childhood where no one came.

Decades later, now a successful health care practitioner and entrepreneur, she still has lingering doubts about people showing up for her when it matters most.

We all experience wounding from childhood (and adulthood). Adverse Childhood Experiences (ACEs) have shown that what happens to us in childhood can impact our adult experiences if we don't take time to understand, acknowledge, and heal from those painful events. Being forgotten, ignored, neglected, abandoned, abused, shamed, or embarrassed can have an unhealthy negative influence on our psyche. According to the CDC website, 61 percent of adults have at least one ACE and 16 percent had four or more types of ACEs which can lead to major health issues, including heart disease, stroke, cancer, depression, and substance abuse.[5]

When we take time to pause and be in the present—whether it is a five-minute personal nightly gratitude practice or a three-hour birthday party for a friend that we attend—we think positive thoughts and feel happy feelings. When in that state, the stress levels in the body immediately go down. When stress decreases, there is an increase in dopamine, serotonin, and endorphins—all chemicals that help us feel good. Dopamine is a neurotransmitter known as the happy hormone. Serotonin helps to regulate mood and helps us feel emotionally stable. Endorphins reduce pain and boost pleasure. Brain science supports the claims that people should celebrate regularly and often![6]

One of the messages I share with my entrepreneurial coaching clients is that other people want to see us succeed. When we succeed, others experience happiness and joy because they feel a connection to us. When we celebrate successes, our clients and colleagues make the association that we are hard-working, smart, and trustworthy. We naturally gravitate to people who are positive and uplifting… and successful!

Rituals and celebrations bring incredible value to our lives, contributing to our overall well-being.

Part Two
Life's Milestone Transitions

When reflecting on life, I imagine there are moments in time that stand still. Those experiences that demarcate "life before X" and "life after X."

Perhaps it is graduating from college, getting married, having a baby, starting a business, getting divorced, the death of a loved one, a major illness, or a big move requiring a complete starting over.

Sometimes these moments may be marked with ritual—a ceremony or party or gathering to acknowledge a change—but other times, life simply moves on and then we look back and wonder what just happened.

Taking time to be intentional with our big transitions—preparing for them, navigating them, and reflecting upon them afterward—helps us to be more emotionally and spiritually in tune with the divine flow of life. As we have seen, part of being human is living in cycles and doing endings and beginnings over and over. Life is constantly evolving, and it is important to mark the passages in meaningful ways. Doing this in community and being witnessed by others who love and care for us is part of what makes life feel rich and fulfilling.

The next section presents inspiration, stories, and practical ideas for how to create Sacred Celebrations for big milestone transitions.

Chapter Six
Welcoming New Life

Babies bring so much joy into the world! With their innocence, laughter, and curiosity, they help us to see the world with fresh eyes and a new perspective. Babies are fully present and offer unconditional love. While babies may cry to get their needs met (when they are hungry or need a diaper change for example), they also inspire adults to cry happy tears of joy when they first arrive in the world and then at different stages along their developmental journey. Celebrating new life is usually a tremendous joy for parents, grandparents, siblings, friends, and extended family members. Sometimes the celebration or ritual can occur before the baby arrives, sometimes afterward, and sometimes there may be both a celebration before *and* after.

Before the Baby Arrives

Traditional rituals like the baby shower, the more modern "baby sprinkle" (a smaller shower sometimes given for a second or third child), or a gender-reveal party are fun ways to help a mother-to-be and her partner celebrate the arrival of their baby.

But if looking to create a gathering that feels more like a sacred ritual or celebration, consider planning a Mother Blessing gathering. The origins of this ritual that celebrates a woman's transition into motherhood come from the Navajo sacred ceremony known as a "blessingway". A Mother Blessing occurs while the mother is pregnant and is designed to help nurture the soon-to-be-mother. The goal is to empower the mother and give her courage, support, and inspiration as she prepares for her transition to motherhood.

A mother can plan her own Mother Blessing or a friend or relative can plan it for her. It is important to invite only women who will uplift and support her. So, chances are good the invitation list may be a bit smaller than a traditional baby shower guest list might be. No need for any Negative Nellies at this event or any women who would share their nightmare labor and delivery stories. Keep it focused on the closest friends and relatives who will be positive, encouraging, and uplifting.

I first attended a Mother Blessing for my girlfriend Angi who was the first one of our group of friends to have a baby. She, a fiery redhead, has a flair for the dramatic, often dressing in colorful vintage clothing and dripping with Southern charm—her mom, a Georgia native.

She lives in Asheville, North Carolina where many residents are very mindful of connection to nature and Mother Earth and where there is a deep spiritual connection to the land and to the community. One of her friends had offered to host a traditional baby shower for her, and instead, Angi asked if she would be willing to cocreate a Mother Blessing. She had attended one at Sewanee where she went to college and it was so memorable, she wanted to create her own.

Participants at a Mother Blessing take turns sharing their blessings for the mother-to-be. I remember there were about twenty-five of us and there was a very long piece of orange ribbon—because orange is Angi's favorite color—that stretched all the way around the room, connecting us all to one another. We each held on to a section and took turns sharing our thoughts and our hearts with Angi. The women who were already mothers shared their best motherly advice. Those of us who were not mothers shared our wishes, hopes, and dreams for the sweet baby girl growing in her belly.

Angi told me later that she received several meaningful gifts including poetry, art, and jewelry. One of her friends gave her three stones—carnelian representing love, quartz for protection, and jade for strength and resilience—to support her journey into motherhood.

She recalled, "I carried them with me to the hospital in a medicine bag that another older woman friend had given me—I kept it around my neck as I gave birth. It had good juju. Those are qualities that a woman needs going into labor and delivery. I kept thinking about how those qualities were what I wanted to embody. It was a way to bring all those women and their blessings with me."

At the end of the ritual, we were all given a candle. When Angi went into labor, there was a phone tree (that was before the days of texting!) already established to notify everyone that she was in labor. Everyone got a call that said, "Light your candle and start thinking about and praying for Angi."

Traditional Elements to Consider for a Mother Blessing Ceremony

Each Mother Blessing is unique; incorporate whatever elements feel good for the gathering of women. Some suggestions include:

- **Pampering**—Giving the pregnant mom hand, head, and foot massages is a lovely way for her to feel pampered and for her to have some hands-on love from her closest friends and family members. A saltwater foot soak bath or anointing with essential oils is also nice (just be sure to check which ones may not be safe during pregnancy).

- **Sharing Circle**—Participants can share blessings and prayers for the mother and for the baby; they can sing or read poems or other inspirational writing.

- **Decorating the Mom-To-Be's Belly**—This can be done with regular paint or with mehndi (ink from the henna plant often used in Hindu rituals) or by creating a belly cast with plaster and then decorating that (again, double check for safety and only the best and highest quality ingredients should be used!) Angi had her belly painted with mehndi and all of her women friends spoke words of wisdom and showered her with words of love and affirmation as they painted on her belly. What a rich experience for any pregnant mama to have!

- **Ribbon Connection**—This can be done during the sharing circle. Take a long piece of ribbon and pass it throughout the group and have each woman wrap the ribbon around her wrist. This symbolizes the connection among the women in the room.

- **Bead Ceremony**—Each guest brings a special bead and shares the significance of it with the mom-to-be who can make a necklace out of the beads to wear during the rest of her pregnancy and/or during labor and delivery to remind her of the community of love that is supporting her.

- **Stone Painting**—Everyone who attends can paint a decorative rock for the mom-to-be to then place around her home that will remind her of her strength as she prepares to bring new life into the world.

- **Flower Crowns**—Make one for the mom-to-be and even invite guests to make one as well. Flowers are always festive and feminine.

- **Candles**—A special candle can burn in the middle of the circle during circle time and then the mother can take this candle with her to burn during her labor and delivery. Each participant can also be given a small candle to take home with them and then when the mother goes into labor, a phone tree or text string is activated, and everyone burns their candles at home and says prayers for the mom for a smooth and safe arrival of the baby.

- **Food**—Offer nourishing, yummy food as part of a celebratory feast. Either the host can provide, or everyone can be asked to bring a potluck dish.

After the Baby Arrives

In many traditions, there are various types of baby blessings. Some Christians practice infant baptism. Jewish families celebrate a *bris* for baby boys. Naming ceremonies are cause for celebration in some Native American, Hindu, and Muslim traditions. Some families opt for a more casual "sip and see" party which is a small gathering for parents to introduce their baby to their friends and family all at once.

Our dear friends Sara and Brian were both raised in the Catholic Church but had not attended regularly as adults. When their daughter, Ayla, was born, they wanted to celebrate her arrival with a spiritual ceremony, and they attended a meeting for new parents at their local Catholic Church. They quickly realized that their vision of a spiritual dedication focused on the blessing and welcoming of an infant into the world was very different from the Church's approach to baptism as an annulment of sins.

They decided to create an intimate, unique ceremony that felt more aligned with how they wanted to celebrate their daughter's arrival into the world. They contacted me, and together with my husband, we discussed what was important for Ayla's special day. They knew it had to involve family, be outdoors, and feel joyful.

Part Two

The celebration was held in a labyrinth next to a magical cottage in Tallahassee, Florida called The Lichgate House. The cottage and the labyrinth were surrounded by a wildflower field and a towering stand of majestic oak trees that are famous in the Tallahassee landscape. The further we stepped into the property, the more our shoulders relaxed, and we felt an almost ethereal quality to the land.

I welcomed everyone to Ayla's spiritual dedication and shared our intentions for the day. I invited and encouraged family members and close friends to enter the labyrinth in silence and while walking, to meditate on their love and adoration for baby Ayla. When everyone reached the center of the labyrinth, they fanned out and formed a semi-circle.

Sara and Brian brought Ayla into the middle where we had placed a small bird bath that doubled as a baptismal font for a water blessing. Her parents were beaming, and baby Ayla was all smiles, too, as I dipped a rose into the water and caressed her head with the wet petals while sharing a simple prayer of celebration for her arrival, her presence, and her light in the world. At that point, Eric read a beautiful Irish blessing that Sara and Brian had chosen, and then we opened the circle and invited attendees to share their thoughts and words Quaker style.

One by one, Ayla's aunts and uncles and grandparents shared their love and prayers, blessings, and good wishes for the first grandchild in the family. There were tears of joy, and the profound love for this child was palpable among the entire group. Ayla is a little Leo baby and her golden hair and blue eyes sparkled as she was lavished with love and adoration.

Years later, Sara recalled, "Brian and I felt satisfied, fulfilled, and uplifted. We wanted it to be a celebration of her life, and as we welcomed her spirit, all agreed to take care of her as best we can. It was a gorgeous day surrounded by family and friends. That was a closer-to-God experience than any other traditional baptism we've ever attended."

In this example, it is easy to see that designing rituals doesn't have to be complicated. Take elements from experiences in other places and create a recipe that works best. In this case, the magical setting, the intimate gathering of their closest relatives and friends, and three simple blessings—a water blessing, an Irish blessing, and blessings and prayers from attendees—combined to make for a memorable celebration for all.

What a gift it was to have the opportunity to facilitate Ayla's spiritual dedication because just four months later we adopted our daughter Riley. When it was time for us to decide how we wanted to welcome her into the spiritual community, we had a direct experience that inspired and guided us.

Community is especially important for new parents because having a brand-new baby to care for is both emotional and overwhelming. Celebrating a baptism, baby blessing, or spiritual dedication is a powerful way to help parents feel supported, uplifted, and not alone on the journey of parenthood. When they are reminded that there is a vast network of family and friends available to them, they embrace the concept of *it takes a village* to raise a child.

Riley arrived so quickly that we had no time to prepare. We call her our "thirty-six-hour pregnancy" because we got the initial phone call on a cold, blustery Saturday morning in January at 4:30 a.m., and by Sunday afternoon at 4:30 p.m., we were checking into the hospital with her and brought her home the next day. We were in total and complete shock, and so were our friends and family. She did not have a room, and we did not have the first diaper, bottle, or a baby onesie.

In the two months after she arrived, our amazing friends hosted four separate baby showers for us. Showering people with gifts is helpful and very practical, especially for new parents. Shifting into caregiving mode 24/7 is a shock for anybody and having support along the way is critical.

Part Two

We were living in Tallahassee, Florida when Riley was born, but some of our best friends in the world were in Asheville, North Carolina, where Eric and I met and married. We couldn't wait to introduce our sweet bundle of joy to our tight-knit community in the mountains.

Our friends conspired to throw a party for our little family when Riley was about six months old. Our minister friend, Barbara Brady, facilitated a simple but deeply meaningful baby blessing ceremony at the event. Hosted in the shady front yard of Eileen and Lars's charming 1920s bungalow, there were cocktails and hors d'oeuvres, and Riley smiled, giggled, and cooed as she was passed from friend to friend. She was born an extrovert, and even as a baby, she was nourished and inspired by being in a big group of people.

At the appointed time, Barbara gathered everyone in a circle, walked around with a bowl of smooth gray river rocks, and invited everyone to take one. One by one she encouraged people to go around the circle and share their thoughts and blessings for baby Riley.

One of my favorite recollections is a friend saying, "May you grow up to be who YOU were meant to be, not who your parents think you *should* be." A powerful prayer indeed.

After the ceremony, everyone placed their rocks, then charged with their love and blessings, into a little bowl with colorful hearts scattered about it that Barbara had chosen specifically for this occasion.

Now that Riley is old enough, she understands the bowl of rocks are her "love rocks" (she named them) and she knows that Mommy and Daddy's friends and family sent her so much love and so many prayers and blessings for a happy, healthy life. If she is ever sad or feeling blue, she knows she can pick up a love rock and hold it and she can connect to their love, energy, and vitality.

Two months after the event, we had Riley baptized in our home church. It was a beautiful celebration that our minister invited us to

Chapter Six: Welcoming New Life

take part in planning. After the church service, we invited close friends and family members back to our home and we repeated the baby blessing circle. With Barbara's help, we gave a script to our friends, Shannon and Kevin, who then facilitated a similar sharing of love and blessings for Riley with the exact same rocks. They became doubly imbued with good juju.

Then, when Riley turned two, her grandparents hosted a Tree Dedication celebration at our family farm in Pinehurst, North Carolina. It was a beautiful day, and several dozen relatives and friends were invited for a picnic and the dedication ritual of a white oak tree planted in her honor. Riley's Lulu (grandmother) read a beautiful poem about a mighty oak tree and delivered a powerful dedication to Riley reminding her that she's now part of a line of several generations of strong men and women. Every year when we go to visit the farm, it is fun to see how Riley's tree has grown.

Things to consider when planning a baby blessing:

- **Choose a facilitator.** It's helpful to have one person facilitate the gathering. It doesn't need to be a minister, simply someone who values the sacred expression of love and celebration that is inherent in a baby blessing.

- **Invite sacred words and blessings.** People can speak off the cuff, or they can read a poem, share a quote, or read other prepared remarks. At Riley's baby blessing, her grandmother Ciddy wrote a sweet and silly poem that everyone adored! Everyone expresses themselves differently so some helpful guidelines without too many limitations would be beneficial.

- **Incorporate nature elements.** When introducing earth, fire, water, and air into any ritual, the concept of balance is evoked which is critical for living a happy and healthy life. Water often represents flow and fertility, candles represent passion and creativity, rocks represent being grounded and stability, and incense represents spirituality.

- **Denote a physical container.** It is helpful to have a box, a bowl, or other container to take home any keepsakes. For example, if participants write a blessing, they could be placed in a pretty decoupage box for reading later.

For Adopted Children

As both an adult adoptee and as an adoptive mother, I understand the importance of ritual and celebration for families impacted by adoption.

Adoption is a unique way of creating a family, filled with both joy and sorrow. It's an imperfect system built on loss: the birth mother places her child for adoption, or the child ends up in the foster care system. The baby or child loses access to his or her biological family, and the adoptive parents (often, not always) experience the grief of infertility and choose to create their family through adoption.

The bright side is that children find forever families, infertile couples are able to become parents and create the family they longed for, and a small degree of consolation may go to the birth parent knowing that their child will be cherished and cared for when they were unable to parent.

"Gotcha Days" are important annual celebrations, especially for families that adopt children when they are older. Some people celebrate their Gotcha Day on the date when they first meet their child, and others celebrate it when the family union is legalized. For many families, the original Gotcha Day occurs in a courtroom for a domestic adoption and in an orphanage for an international adoption. For some children adopted internationally, their birthdates are not necessarily exactly known, so celebrating their Gotcha Day is a firm day for the family to acknowledge.

I was placed with my adoptive parents when I was only two weeks old, and we brought our adopted daughter home from the hospital when she was only two days old. We never celebrated

Chapter Six: Welcoming New Life

Gotcha Days, but instead, made a special point to recognize my birth mother and my daughter's birth mother on our birthdays.

I still recall sitting at the kitchen table with my mom when I was about ten years old on my birthday, and she said, "There is a beautiful young woman out there thinking of you today, just as she thinks of you every year on your birthday."

Mine was a closed adoption so that revelation had a big impact on me, and I started to think more of my birth mother as a real person rather than a fantasy.

My daughter's adoption, on the other hand, is somewhat open. We met her birth mother in the hospital and communicated with her for two years, exchanging texts and photographs, until she dropped contact with us when Riley was about two years old. Riley has a photograph of her birth mother on her bedside altar, and we talk about her all the time. She knows her birth mother's name and a little bit about her.

When we adopted Riley, there were all sorts of celebrations. We were given four baby showers. We had about fifteen people with us at the courthouse when her adoption was finalized, sharing cupcakes together in the hallway. I distinctly recall the postman arriving on my doorstep with yet another package about three months after Riley was born and saying to me with incredulity, "Mrs. Barbour, I haven't missed a day of bringing you a package in about three months!" The non-stop celebration of our little bundle of joy was so good for our souls after gut-wrenching years of infertility and wondering if we would ever become parents.

I recall my mother watching in disbelief from afar and how gobsmacked she was by the attention surrounding our daughter's arrival.

One day she said to me, "We never had any of this when we got you. The social worker showed up on our doorstep when you were two weeks old and said, 'Here she is' and that was that. There were

Part Two

no showers, no celebrations, and just a handful of friends sent gifts."

Times were different in the 1970s. Fortunately, times have changed, and adoptive parents and their children are regularly feted as they make the step in becoming forever families.

One of my high school classmates, Debra Depass Jones, shared the following with me. "We were matched with Olivia when she was seven months old and received our first pictures. We traveled to China when she was ten months old. When we got her, she had about nine layers of clothes on, which is key to our Gotcha Day celebration. Typically, on her Gotcha Day, we order Chinese food, look at the pictures, watch a video that my husband compiled of us meeting her and then take out the box of clothes and talk about what order they were on her and how we laughed because we never thought we'd get to the baby in all those layers. Sometimes we talk about the whole process and sometimes we look at other pictures but sometimes not. We let her guide us in the conversation. Sometimes she asks about the foster mom which is hard because we just don't have a ton of answers. And sometimes (more on her birthday) she asks about her biological mom and dad. This is also hard because there are so few details we know. All we can do is encourage and support her curiosity."

Angie and Paul Wierzbicki live in Houston, Texas. Dear friends of ours, they had a long and rocky road to parenthood just like we had. I'll never forget attending Angie's fortieth birthday party (quite a ritual celebration in and of itself) and towering, but teddy-bear-like Paul, bursting into the room wildly waving a piece of paper with two photographs on it saying, "We're going to be parents! These are going to be our daughters!"

They were both beaming with joy, and there wasn't a dry eye in the house after that announcement. Two years later, we attended their Gotcha Day celebration, which was on the official day they adopted daughters JoLee and Symphony. They had shared the

Chapter Six: Welcoming New Life

private courthouse experience with just immediate family but then hosted a big "Worth the Wait" themed pizza and cupcake party for dozens of friends from all parts of their lives who had supported them through the entire adoption process.

I asked my friend, Donna Konuch, to share her version of their Gotcha Day celebration:

"My husband and I were raising our twin boys Nathan and Alex, when at the age of five, Nathan began to ask us out of the blue, 'Where is our sister? She is already born. Why isn't she here?' My husband and I just looked at each other in shock because we had often talked about the possibility of adoption and then for one reason or another would talk ourselves out of it. We never discussed this idea in front of the children.

"Nathan, who had always been my more spiritual child, would repeat those sentences to us a few more times, and once that happened, my husband and I considered that a sign from God and began an adoption process. We again did not discuss this decision with the boys because of their young age, but as soon as we started the paperwork on an adoption, Nathan stopped asking the questions.

"A year later, after various international adoption hurdles, we traveled to China with our then six-year-old twin boys to pick up their sister. Jade-Rose was five, almost six, when she joined our family, and seven months out of the year I can claim to have triplets versus twins, because all three kids are the same age!

"On the very first day with Jade-Rose in our family, we went out for ice cream. A common event for six-year-old American boys, but Jade-Rose had never seen ice cream before, let alone tasted it. She displayed so much joy as we celebrated her over soft vanilla ice cream cones that it became one of our family traditions. Every year, we go out for soft-serve ice cream on August 23rd to celebrate Gotcha Day or what we now call Jade Day! It is undeniably one of our most significant family traditions, and one we hold precious and dear to our hearts, just like that little girl."

Here are some simple ways to celebrate a Gotcha Day with family and friends:

- **Throw a party!** Kids love parties, and whether it's a dinner party with close family and friends or a big bash with dozens of people, it is a wonderful way to celebrate a precious little one. Let the child choose the theme or get inspired by Sarah Kay Hoffman's blog where she suggests a few cute ideas including Worth the Wait, Wishes Come True, Precious Cargo, or Born in Our Hearts.

- **Create annual traditions.** Perhaps start the day with a special blessing and reviewing photographs or stories from the original Gotcha Day. With international adoptions, it can be a special day for the family to prepare food and listen to music from the child's country of birth. If the family has an open adoption, it may be a special day to spend time with the child's birth parents, share a phone call with them, or write a letter to them.

- **Design an honoring ritual.** Emotions can be high on a Gotcha Day as the young, adopted person takes time to think about their birth mother and birth family, and keenly feels the separation from them. It may be a time to have a simple ritual of lighting candles and saying prayers and blessings in honor of the birth family, and also for the family to continue to grow in love as a forever family.

Remember that emotions can run high and that celebrations will vary from year to year. Two years ago, thanks to Ancestry.com, we were reunited with Riley's biological father, and he now has become a regular part of her birthday celebrations. She loves learning about her Mexican and Japanese heritage from him.

Donna mentioned that when her Chinese daughter was younger, she loved incorporating aspects of Chinese culture into her Gotcha Day celebrations but now that she is an Americanized teenager, she is less interested. As a child grows and evolves, they may experience different feelings about their adoption, and it is important to let *them* direct what they would like to do.

Chapter Seven
Birthdays

"On the night you were born, the moon smiled with such wonder that the stars peeked in to see you and the night wind whispered, 'Life will never be the same.' Because there has never been anyone like you... ever in the world."

Nancy Tillman
On the Night You Were Born [7]

Whether we have given birth or attended a birth, we know what a sacred and holy experience it is. This is the transition from the unborn to the born, from the safety of the dark fertile womb of our mothers, to the lights and chaos of living fully in human form. It is the moment when we take our first breath and say to the world, "Here I am!"

Each year, when we celebrate the anniversary of our birth, it's an opportunity to remember who we are—our essence, our God-given talents and gifts. We sometimes disconnect from our true selves with our human nature and propensity for focusing on the mundane, and birthdays are an opportunity to realign and live in integrity with who we are.

Birthdays are probably the most recognized celebration that we have in our Western culture. Some people throw lavish parties, others have dinner with a few friends, and still others are happy to sit home on the couch watching Netflix and log on to Facebook periodically to see the ubiquitous Happy Birthday messages. Some people love the idea of being given a surprise party with a gazillion friends, and others cringe at the thought of being thrust into the spotlight.

Historians have different ideas about when birthdays were first celebrated but it seems that the Egyptians, the Romans, and the Chinese were some of the earliest cultures to record birthday celebrations. In Egypt, when pharaohs became crowned, it was believed they became gods, and that coronation date was considered their birthday. In ancient Rome, not only were people celebrated for their beginnings, but so were temples and cities.[8] And no matter where you live, birthdays and birth times are still important for creating people's astrology and Human Design charts.

My mom grew up in an orphanage in the 1930s and 1940s and as an adult, she never wanted a fuss made about her birthday. My guess is that when she was little, no one cared to honor, recognize, or celebrate her unique light in the world.

I honestly don't know because she never talked about it. However, I suspect that she wanted me to have the exact opposite experience, and as a result, she made sure to make *my* birthday a big deal when I was little. Sometimes it was just preparing my favorite dinner (thick, juicy lamb chops), other times it was gathering a small group of friends at a restaurant.

I distinctly remember my tenth birthday party at the Ancient Mariner, a nautical-themed restaurant and bar that my family frequented every weekend in our small hometown of Ridgefield,

Connecticut. They sectioned off a corner of the restaurant just for me and my friends, and I remember carefully choosing a glass figurine party favor for each of my party guests based on what I thought their favorite animal was. Whatever the celebration, there was always cake and presents, and Mom always let me know I was cherished.

When I was in the early stages of studying the ancient healing tradition of shamanism and being mentored by my Peruvian-trained shamanic practitioner mentor, Marna McGee, she introduced me to the term, *ayni*—an Andean term for "sacred reciprocity." This is the idea that there is a give-and-take to all aspects of the universe: "what goes around comes around" and "do unto others as you would have them do unto you." Many of the world's faith systems embrace this concept as well. It is often known as The Golden Rule (or the law of reciprocity) and it appears clearly in Buddhism, Christianity, Hinduism, Judaism, Taoism, and the majority of the world's religions.

It was in this sacred exchange with Marna, where I heard The Golden Rule (something I've learned over and over again in my life) in a slightly different form where it dawned on me that this is *exactly* why celebrating our birthdays is so critical. The gift of life, the gift of being born, is something to be grateful for. Being in human form, designed by our great Creator, is a sacred gift. So every year, when the anniversary of your birth comes around, it's important to say, "Thank you for giving me life."

For my fiftieth birthday, it felt important to honor this new decade with fanfare. I love birthdays (my own and others) at any time, but milestone birthdays that end in zero seem like especially important times to not only pause and celebrate the passage of time and the wisdom earned but also revel in the love of family and friends. We were living in Texas at the time and had a wonderful group of friends there, but I also had some lifelong friends who lived in North Carolina. Originally, I wanted those folks to fly out to Texas and join the party there, but then I learned that Oprah was going to be in Charlotte the week after my birthday, so it was very clear that two separate celebrations were in order!

For the first celebration, we invited friends to join us in whimsical Wimberley, a small town in the beautiful Hill Country region of Texas, just south of Austin. There is a magical and mystical quality to the land with its rolling hills, spring-fed rivers, and diverse vegetation. The Wildflower Inn was the perfect retreat-style space for all of us, complete with an organic garden, hiking trails, a labyrinth in the woods, peacocks who strolled around the property, and an outdoor fire pit with twinkly lights strung in the trees.

On the first night, as people were arriving, I scheduled a local energy healer to come and offer intuitive readings for anyone interested. We ate gourmet pizza and an espresso chocolate torte from my favorite caterers in Asheville, North Carolina that I had shipped overnight just for the occasion.

We structured the days so people could choose to either do group activities or couple activities, or groups of friends could go off on their own for a few hours. We had most of our meals together and all of us gathered to go to the gorgeous Wimberley Blue Hole, a spring-fed swimming area with crystal-clear waters. Afterward, some people went hiking, others went shopping, and still others simply enjoyed having quiet time and space to read and nap. On Saturday night, we converted the living room to accommodate a 1980s dance party thanks to a great playlist created by my friend Charles. The non-dancers enjoyed drinks around a bonfire out on the patio underneath the starry skies.

My girlfriends know that I value ritual and offered to create a special women's sacred gathering. On Saturday morning, they decorated the little yoga barn that was on the property with twinkling white lights and created a beautiful circle for us to sit in. One by one, the women went around the room and shared three things with me. They had each chosen a word that they felt described me, they each had selected a crystal that they wanted to give me, and they all told stories of our friendship, how we met, and how they valued our connection.

I was given a specially decorated box, and all the crystals and words of affirmation were placed in it. The box sits on an altar in my office to this day! When I close my eyes, I can take myself back to that moment, and see myself seated in the circle with those beautiful, shiny, sparkly women gathered round to celebrate me. It was the ultimate gift that they gave me—and that I gave myself— by allowing myself to receive such heartfelt words of affirmation and love.

The following week, I flew to Charlotte and met five of my best girlfriends for our big Oprah adventure. I had attended one of Oprah's events in Texas several years prior, and I knew she put on an incredible performance. The vibe was high, the inspiration was palpable, and it was electric to be in an arena with 10,000 women (and a few good men) trying to live their best lives.

Then on Sunday morning, my besties planned a powerful ritual for me. What's interesting is that they didn't consult with my Texas friends, but there were similar qualities in both circles.

There was an elaborate altar set up in the middle of the room. One by one, the women went around and lit a candle and shared with me their experience of knowing me and our friendship. They each gave me a small crystal or a talisman to remind me of my power and to invite me to embrace my crone years. Then they took time to ask me a series of questions. "What do you want to create in this next phase of your life? What are your hopes and dreams? What is your big vision for this next decade?" They invited me to set powerful intentions by speaking my answers aloud, and they affirmed my commitments and helped me expand upon them.

These women have known me for decades, so when I shared an idea, they said, "And what else? How can you make it bigger? How can you step more fully into this vision of what's possible?" Then they captured everything I said out loud in writing, and at the end, they went around the room and read back to me what I said I wanted.

It is one thing to speak desires out loud, it's another to hear them reflected back by the voices of friends and cheerleaders who love you unconditionally and who believe that you truly can make your dreams come true.

At the end of our time together, we cranked up some music and danced. And before we left our weekend together, they presented me with a beautiful journal that captured all of the ideas, intentions, wishes, and dreams spoken that weekend (they had been taking notes on Post-its and plastered them into the journal!) so I have a keepsake and touchstone to refer back to when I'm doubting myself and need some inspiration from my girlfriends.

I believe that celebrating birthdays or allowing friends and family to celebrate with us, is life-affirming. When you dismiss or ignore your birthday, it's almost as though you are ignoring—or even rejecting—the gift of your precious life. By not receiving love from people around you, you are effectively putting a stopper on the flow of abundance and the recognition of your uniqueness. And when others dismiss or ignore your birthday, it can be painful because you feel that you aren't seen or worthy of taking up space in this world.

Being reminded of our inner divine spark is a beautiful thing. Birthdays can be a time of celebrating our strengths, gifts, and talents, and they can show us just how much love surrounds us. Sometimes we forget, and it is good to remember.

But if you don't want your birthday celebration to be all about you, you can try turning the birthday tradition upside down, and instead, host a party in honor of your friends and loved ones.

Naana Jefferson lives in Sugar Land, Texas, and is an attorney, wife, and mother. She is a regal woman with a smile that can light up a room with even more high wattage since the birth of her first

Chapter Seven: Birthdays

child. This is her story about how she made her thirty-seventh birthday extra special:

"For my November birthday a few years ago, I threw a Thanksgiving brunch for a few ladies who had made an impression in my life over the years. I sent formal invitations and the venue printed menus. I gave them all a rose in honor of my mother (Rose) who is deceased, and I danced to 'Flowers' by India Arie as a tribute to them. My middle school teacher was there, as was my manager from one of my jobs many years ago, a 'mother' from the church, and others. It was beautiful seeing them interact with each other, and the love in the room was the best gift ever."

She went on to say, "I often think of my mother and the void of not having her in my life since her passing. But I've been grateful that God has allowed me to look back and realize that while I did not have a mother or a mother figure, He did allow certain women to cross my path and deposit something within me. I wanted to let them know that I was grateful for what they shared with me."

Isn't that a lovely and meaningful twist on the traditional birthday party? Throwing a party in honor of friends instead of them planning one for you? Singing or dancing for loved ones instead of them singing the birthday song to you? Giving them gifts instead of receiving them?

Because this book is about encouraging celebration beyond just the typical cake and candles, happy birthday song and presents, let's talk about how to add elements of presence and intention to birthday gatherings.

Celebrating Yourself

Here are several ways to make birthdays more meaningful and richer:

- **Create a vision board.** Using magazines, scissors, glue, and poster paper, create a board that visually represents what you desire for the year ahead. It is a great tool to help focus and clarify your vision about your deepest desires. For almost twenty years, I have been using annual vision boards to guide my way. My birthday happens to be in January, so, sometime between the new year and my birthday, I create a vision board for myself. The gift of time and creativity is wonderful, but the resulting artwork becomes a map or guideline for the year ahead. It is a visual reminder of all of the things I say that I want to accomplish or experience in the coming year, and every time I see it, it reinforces those messages.

- **Write down your goals and dreams**. You can capture these in your journal, make a list and post it on the bulletin board in your office, or write a letter to your future self describing what accomplishments you want to be celebrating in one year's time. When you think about goals, you engage the creative right brain, but writing them down engages the logic-based left brain too, thus creating a whole-brain approach to accomplishing your goals.

- **Engage in a "Year in Review" with some close friends**. Reflect on the previous year and what you have learned, and then speak with intention about what you want to create in the coming year. Don Miguel Ruiz writes in his book, *The Four Agreements,* "The word is not just a sound or a written symbol. The word is a force; it is the power you have to express and communicate, to think, and thereby to create the events in your life. You can speak. What other animal on the planet can speak? The word is the most powerful tool you have as a human; it is the tool of magic." [9] Our words are significant and having them witnessed by close friends as you set your intentions makes the experience even more powerful.

- **Create a tradition that becomes an annual ritual**. Take your birthday off from work and schedule a day date for yourself or with a friend. Eat dinner at the same restaurant with your family every year. Make a special meal (or ask that it be made for you) that is a rare treat. In Mexico, children celebrate with piñatas. In Jamaica, friends douse the birthday girl/boy with flour. In China, many people celebrate two birthdays—one on the solar calendar and one on the lunar calendar. In Vietnam, everyone celebrates their birthdays together on New Year's Day.

Celebrating Others

Here are some creative gift ideas to make a birthday celebration for someone else more meaningful:

- **Written love notes.** Several people I talked with who have helped plan a party for someone else gathered letters and handwritten birthday wishes for the guest of honor. This definitely seems more common for the older set—people in their sixties, seventies, and eighties—but certainly could be appropriate for younger people. It is especially valuable if you can gather notes from people representing all stages of a person's life—family, current friends, friends from high school and college, neighbors, work colleagues, people from different cities they have lived in, etc.

- **Words of affirmation**. These can be funny or serious. Ask guests to share a favorite memory or story of the birthday person. It is fun to relive memories, but it also helps the group that is gathered to know more about the guest of honor. People can also be invited to share their favorite qualities or characteristics of the person, or it could go really silly, like my friend Deanna Mims in Tallahassee, Florida—she hosted a party where guests were prompted to answer the question "If Deanna were a donut, what kind would she be?"

- **Gather photos.** Images of loved ones evoke emotions like nothing else can. Seeing snapshots from childhood, vacations, graduations, family reunions, and other special events transports people back in space and time and helps everyone relive the joy of the moment. With online programs like Snapfish, Shutterfly, Mixbook, and others, compiling a keepsake photo book that will be cherished is easy.

Get your creative juices flowing and get inspired with these fun birthday rituals and celebrations that have been shared with me:

For her mother-in-law's eightieth birthday, Nicole Rathjen mailed out custom '80s birthday postcards to her mother-in-law's old friends and classmates a few months ahead of time. They wrote memories and notes to her and then mailed them back. At her party, Nicole wrapped them together as a gift so she could go through them and read their well wishes. Her mother-in-law loved it!

Nicole Guillory shared a touching story about a special dance she shared with her dad. "Every year on my birthday for as long as I can remember, my dad and I would stay up until 1:04 a.m. because that's when I was born, and he would dance with me. I looked forward to that birthday dance every year. As I got older, and my dad was not by my side at the turn of the clock, I always continued the tradition of our birthday dance. In college, my best friends would do me the honor of my special dance, then significant others, and now my husband dances with me every year (even though we don't always make it to 1:04 a.m. *haha*). Now that my dad has died, I really miss him, but I will continue to honor his memory and the very best gift he has ever given me. We have passed the tradition on to our daughter for her birthday."

"For my grandmother's eightieth, we had all of the family and friends hide in the upstairs of a restaurant downtown," recounts

Ashley Mitchell. "My mom and dad brought Gram to dinner and every sixty seconds one of us walked downstairs and sat down at a table. Eventually the whole restaurant was filled with her family and friends, and she didn't even realize it. Then when she started to look around, she noticed we were all there. It was so great to see the astonishment on her face!"

Tippy Amick is a fun-loving, retired, team-building consultant who loves engaging others in a group setting. "I asked my birthday party attendees to entertain me for five minutes. People wrote and read poems and songs, some acted out skits, and others told stories. It was a magical event!"

"My boys went to a Montessori preschool," shared Mollie Eardley. "They do a cute birthday ceremony. The kids sit in a circle around a candle representing the sun and the birthday child walks around the candle/sun carrying a globe. They walk around once for each year, usually while the parent reads out one thing about them during that year of their lives. The children love it, and the parents appreciate being part of this special ritual."

Birthdays can be difficult for some people. Friends have told me they don't enjoy being the center of attention or in the spotlight. Some people think that celebrating their own birthday can be perceived as boastful and self-centered. Others don't like surprises and don't like the feeling of not being in control if someone else plans a birthday gathering. Adopted people or children in foster care may have a hard time acknowledging their birthday if it makes them sad to feel separated from their biological family.

Often, traumatic experiences in childhood have shaped our outlook as adults. Think about the seven-year-old who invites her entire class to her birthday party, and nobody comes. That girl grows up to be an adult who never wants to have a birthday party for fear of being rejected or neglected again. Or the eleven-year-old who ends up in the emergency room because he broke his collarbone playing football at his birthday party. That boy may grow up to avoid birthday parties, his own and others, because he has a fear of getting hurt.

Danielle Metcalfe-Chenail is a Canadian author, historian, and mother. We became friends when we lived in the same neighborhood in Houston, and I learned that she likes to keep birthday celebrations low-key. At first, I thought it was because she tends to be more introverted than I am. But as our friendship deepened over the years, she revealed that birthdays are stressful because she grew up in a family that didn't recognize or celebrate birthdays as a big deal.

Now the mother of two children, Danielle had a powerful healing experience when her nine-year-old son asked for a scavenger hunt birthday party with his friends. She was delighted to witness the children laughing and playing, and her son soaked up the attention and adoration of his friends. When he decided to open all of the gifts in front of his friends, she cringed because she had been taught that was a selfish thing to do.

To her surprise, and eventual delight, the other partygoers *oohed* and *aahed* watching her son open his presents, and then they all immediately started playing with the new toys as a group. It was such a joyful experience to witness, and it helped her embrace a different mindset regarding birthdays for herself and her children moving forward.

Concerns about getting older are another reason why some people might avoid celebrating their birthdays. In our Western society that celebrates youth, vitality, and wrinkle-free faces, it can be hard to embrace getting older. But in some cultures, growing older means growing wiser. It means an elevated status in the community or circle.

In India, elders are the head of the family and are respected for their wisdom and advice. In Korea, elders are highly respected and there are special celebrations for the sixtieth and seventieth birthdays. In Native American communities, elders are revered for their wisdom and knowledge and pass on their learnings through stories to younger members of the tribe.[10]

Consider the benefits of aging. Many are more comfortable in their skin and better equipped to surf the emotional rollercoaster of life. With age often comes financial security or free time without the demands of childcare, child raising, work, and career. A bonus of aging is that most people have had great opportunities to gain wisdom, empathy, compassion for others and have had many lived experiences that add perspective to most situations. There are plenty of reasons to celebrate getting older.

Quiet Ways to Honor Your Day of Birth

If you truly are a minimalist, consider things like lighting a candle, making a list of things you are grateful for from the previous year, writing out your hopes and dreams for the next cycle of life, getting an astrology reading, taking yourself out to lunch or dinner, or buying yourself a small treat.

If your mother is still living, you could call her and thank her for giving you life. If she's not, you could put flowers in her honor near a photo of her or speak out loud to her in your favorite spot in nature and ask that your message be carried to her through the cosmos.

If you still want to spend time with a few friends but don't want a fuss, do what Dallas-based author Jon Malesic does and have a "stealth" birthday where you ask people to get together for dinner or drinks but don't tell them why, or you tell them at the end of your time together. As Jon says, "I want to be with people but don't want them to make a big deal out of the day. Just being in their company is enough of a treat." The key is to find what works for you.

Chapter Eight
Growing Up

As our children grow, they go through many stages and cycles. Kids start school in the fall and complete the academic year at the end of the spring. There are big transitions from elementary to middle school and then again to high school and beyond. Each new ending offers an opportunity for review, learning, and celebration, and then it's on to their next new adventures. In the middle of so many transitions, families also have the opportunity to celebrate major milestones as children grow into young adults.

Coming-of-Age Rituals

Parents often crave meaningful ways to connect with their teenagers so they can help them navigate the sometimes-rocky patches during those adolescent years. Coming-of-age rituals can be a wonderful way to let teenagers know they are seen, heard, and valued for who they are.

If they already have a strong sense of self, a celebration can help to cement positive self-regard for life. If they are unsure of themselves, these formalized gatherings can give them a sense of confidence and purpose, help them to claim their place in the world, and acknowledge the fact that they are going through a time of big transition.

Throughout history, various religions and cultures around the world have engaged in coming-of-age rituals. Some are religious in nature and are designed to deepen a young person's faith. Some relate to the physical changes children go through as they sexually mature from girls into women and boys into men. Others still are designed to develop strength, character, and wisdom. And almost all of them are about encouraging youth to step up and claim responsibility for themselves and for their place in their community.

Here are some examples of traditional coming-of-age ceremonies from around the globe:

In the Jewish religion, a girl will celebrate her bat mitzvah at the age of twelve, and a boy will celebrate his bar mitzvah at thirteen. At this time, the children are considered adults, and as such, are expected to uphold the Jewish commandments and laws.

Confirmation in the Christian faith means to strengthen one's relationship with God. In many Western Catholic, Baptist, and Methodist churches, confirmation for young men and women occurs around age fourteen.

In many Latin American countries, the *quinceañera* celebration is important for girls at age fifteen. In North America, it can be popular for a girl to have a sweet sixteen party. And in aristocratic or upper-class societies in the UK, Australia, and the US, when a young woman is between the ages of sixteen and eighteen, she is introduced as a debutante. These are all designed to introduce a young woman into society.

The Amish and Mennonite communities have a rite of passage for their youth called *Rumspringa*, which roughly translates to "running around." At about the age of sixteen, youth are invited to experience life outside of the traditional confines of their communities, and may experiment with drinking, drugs, driving cars, dressing American, and engaging in other non-traditional activities. It is an opportunity to see if they want to leave their communities of origin, or if they want to stay and commit themselves to the church.

The *Vision Quest* is a rite of passage in many Native American cultures for young men ages fourteen to fifteen entering adulthood. It often involves several days of fasting and solitude in the wilderness, coupled with ceremony and support from elders in the tribe before and after their return. During this time, the young man may experience a vision that will guide him on his purpose in life and in his quest for service to his community.

Coming-of-Age Day (*Seijin no hi*) is a holiday celebrated on the second Monday in January in Japan. Ceremonies are held around the country to celebrate Japanese men and women who have turned twenty—considered the age of majority—within that year.

If you want to design your own coming-of-age ritual for your kids in their teen years, incorporate traditions from the ones mentioned above or design something completely fresh, new, and unique for your family.

Things to consider when designing your gathering:

- **Choose a theme that reflects your child**. If your young teen is artistic, plan a celebration that involves making art. If your child loves nature, plan the celebration at a park incorporating outdoor activities like hiking, fishing, or camping. Whatever you choose, create an inclusive environment that reflects your child's interests and is accessible to as many people as possible.

- **Invite friends and family with intention**. Talk to your teen and find out if they want this to be family, friends, or a mixture of friends and family-type gathering. It doesn't have to be large to be impactful. In fact, the smaller it is, the more intimate the sharing can be, which will facilitate more opportunities for richer conversations.

- **Include a ritual ceremony in the greater celebration**. Similar to a wedding that is a longer affair with several aspects, be sure to have some part of the gathering that is more sacred. For instance, circles are sacred. If the event is held outdoors, perhaps people could sit around a campfire and elders can share their favorite wisdom and stories with the young person coming-of-age.

- **Make sure this is a co-creative experience**. In the e-book *Coming-of-Age Ceremonies*, Jennifer Brimhall suggests that parents and their teens design the coming-of-age ceremony together. She encourages parents to identify what values they want to pass on to their children, and she offers a practical worksheet called "Who I Want to Be" for teens to fill out.

First Day of School Rituals

The beginning and the end of the traditional school year are important bookends to a year in a child's life. So much growth and change occur during an academic year at every level—physically, mentally, emotionally, spiritually, and socially.

Starting off feeling excited and prepared for the unknowns that lay ahead is important. The year is filled with change—new teachers, new classmates, new academic subjects—and sometimes involves moving to a new school.

Simple rituals like getting a fun backpack, gathering school supplies, buying new clothes and shoes, and getting the scoop on teachers, may help a child get excited for what is to come. If they can feel confident and prepared on their first day, it will help to set them up for success in the coming year.

I remember growing up in Connecticut, my mom would always take me to get new clothes at the Stanford Mall. We would pick a day in August and go shopping, have lunch, and usually get an ice cream treat at the end of the day. We would come home exhausted with colorful packages and then I would host a little fashion show for my dad to show him what we got. It was a necessary thing that had to happen (buying clothes because I had outgrown mine) but my parents made it feel special and fun.

If you want to be even more intentional with each grade and your approach to the new school year, do as my friend Kate Lumley, an inspirational artist, does with her three children. They spend time together the night before talking about intentions for the upcoming school year. It is a very simple but meaningful conversation that happens on the same day each year. Rituals do not have to be elaborate or complicated to still have meaning and make an impression.

For younger children, there is a sweet book called *The Kissing Hand* by Audrey Penn, about a mother raccoon comforting her baby raccoon by kissing its paw. In real life, the author witnessed this exchange at a national park where the ranger explained to her it was the parent's way of transferring her scent to the baby raccoon to recall by bringing her paw to her face.

Penn started doing this ritual with her own daughter and then wrote a book about it! It is a super simple but very powerful act to comfort your young son or daughter—especially for children with separation anxiety—each morning as they head to school.

Academic year rituals are also important for parents. The transition from lazy summer days to the structure and discipline of the school year can be an adjustment. I have heard it said that there are two types of parents when children return to the regular school routine of the year: the boohoo variety and the woohoo types. I'll confess to being a little of both. The year that my daughter entered second grade in Texas, I heard about four different restaurants that hosted a "Moms and Mimosas" brunch. And even some schools offer what they call a Boohoo Breakfast for parents after dropping kids off for the first day.

One positive benefit of social media is that it has helped us to really uplevel our public celebration game in all things, from birthdays to anniversaries to special celebrations. This is especially true for the first day of school rituals. Parents take photos of their children holding a sign and wearing their best clothes on their front doorstep. Some decorate with streamers and balloons, others use a fancy chalkboard, and some even buy a large T-shirt with their son or daughter's graduating class on it and have them pose year after year, each time getting just a little bit bigger and filling out the T-shirt!

Capturing these moments in time and sharing them on Facebook and Instagram have become a fun ritual for students and parents alike. Until, of course, they are teenagers and no longer let parents take their photograph! It is also a great way to connect with relatives like grandparents and aunts and uncles who live far away but still want to share in the excitement of yet another new year, another transition, another milestone in growing up!

Graduation Rituals

The endings inherent in our formal education are excellent times to plan meaningful rituals for young people. Graduating from high school, college, or graduate school marks the end of significant chapters in a person's life and are all fantastic reasons to celebrate. It is a time for reflection, relief, release, and pride.

Hard work deserves recognition, especially in our society where people can be reluctant to be in the spotlight. Children and youth receive conflicting messages from parents and teachers. On one hand, they are told "be humble" and "don't brag" and "don't call attention to yourself," but in the media, we have five-year-olds with YouTube channels that focus on opening Easter eggs, and television shows that encourage the me-generation mentality of selfless promotion with disregard to others. Hiding from the spotlight is not productive, nor is excessive self-promotion the pathway to building healthy self-esteem. There is a happy balance somewhere in the middle.

Healthy acknowledgment and celebration are good and appropriate. This is why ritual is so important; it reminds us that many of our successes and accomplishments do not occur in a vacuum, they happen when we are supported, inspired, and guided along the way by teachers, mentors, parents, siblings, friends, and other relatives.

We need to teach our children that it is not only okay to stop, rest, and celebrate, it is good for our health. It boosts our self-esteem and confidence to share the news of achievements, and it allows others to build faith and trust as they see people's natural talents shine.

Traditional graduation festivities often include graduates wearing a cap and gown, marching to the strains of "Pomp and Circumstance," and tossing caps in the air at the end of the commencement ceremony. Often, families gather to acknowledge the accomplishments of the young person they love, and there can be a family meal, a big party, and sometimes presents are given. It's important to recognize these milestone achievements because celebrating success begets more success.

Some high schools have really fun rituals for graduating seniors. These include seniors-only talent shows, painting collegiate logos on the school windows representing their future alma maters, dressing up in cap and gown and returning to their former elementary schools to walk through the halls where the grade schoolers cheer the graduates on. There are a lot of fun and festive rituals that can mark the important occasion of graduation.

During the COVID pandemic we saw creative graduations held outdoors at drive-in movie theaters, large sports stadiums, and car parades with elaborately decorated vehicles that were de rigueur around the world.

More solemn occasions are also an important part of celebration. Some high schools and many colleges offer a special baccalaureate ceremony, which is more religious in nature, in addition to the commencement ceremony. Nursing students say that the pinning ceremony is particularly meaningful as faculty and mentors "pin" students in a heartfelt gathering designed to recognize each student's accomplishment. In medical school, the hooding ceremony is often a highlight for graduates.

When I graduated from The College of William & Mary in Williamsburg, Virginia, on the last day of class seniors were invited to the Wren Building (the oldest academic building in continuous use in the United States) to ring the bell to represent that we had completed our undergraduate education. Then, on commencement day, the graduates joined in the processional across campus starting at the Wren Building, cross the bridge at Crim Dell, and up to the stadium where graduation took place. This path was the exact opposite of the one we walked as incoming freshmen.

Send-Off Rituals

Recognizing our young people who may be entering military service or starting a new job is important too. Throw a boot camp-themed party and invite people to share words of encouragement in a gathering or bring handwritten notes of good luck. For someone entering the workforce, tips and ideas about professional etiquette could be shared along with small gifts like Starbucks gift cards, dry cleaning coupons, and money for gas or public transportation.

Here are some ideas for a festive send-off for any young person who is heading off to college, joining the military, or starting their first job:

- Hold a gathering at one of the person's favorite places. It could be someone's home, a special place in nature, or their beloved ice cream shop.

- Identify the people closest to the young person. Invite them to join in a send-off celebration but let them know it's going to be more than just a party; it will be marked with meaning and intention.

- Invite everyone in attendance to bring a letter, a poem, a song, a photograph, or some other item to give to the young adult. Encourage people to highlight the things that they love and appreciate about this person. Encourage people to keep it fun and practical like creating a College Student Survival Kit complete with useful things like quarters for laundry, stamps to write home, and gift cards to download iTunes music. For a young man or woman headed to basic training, gather inspirational quotes and stories about mental toughness and resilience to help bolster them during the grueling first weeks of training.

- Create a memento box they can keep all these special items in to take with them when they embark on their new journey.

- During the gathering, host a ritual where guests have an opportunity to speak from the heart, read a letter or poem they have written, and shower the young person with positive messages as they prepare to embark on their new journey. For a more spiritual feel, invite the young person to sit in the middle of the room and everyone can have a laying-on-of-the-hands ritual where they place a hand on their body and say a prayer or blessing over them.

Chapter Nine
Weddings

When my beloved Eric and I got married in Asheville, North Carolina in the autumn of 2004, it was fun to plan our wedding because it was a second marriage for both of us. We were relaxed and at ease, and we felt we could toss the etiquette book out the window, much to my mother's chagrin! We both had experienced traditional first weddings in churches with organ music, large wedding parties, and the big white dress, but because we were older, paying for our own wedding, and didn't feel like we had to follow traditions or protocol, we were free to eschew tradition and personalize our wedding day to make it our own.

I wore an iridescent gold dress with purple shoes, we got married outside on a majestic mountaintop, and we walked into the ceremony together where our guests sat in a circle waiting for us. We wrote our own vows, included mention of his beloved golden retriever mix Andy and my three fluffy incorrigible kitty cats, and we didn't have a bridal party. Our minister surprised us by kicking off the ceremony singing the first verse of Frank Sinatra's "Fly Me to the Moon" *a cappella* which gave an ethereal quality to the entire event.

Whether you're getting married for the first time (or not), have a traditional wedding (or not), or have a big wedding (or not), it is possible to design a day that is perfect for you and your partner. There are many wedding traditions that are considered standard... a couple being married in a church or place of worship, the bride wearing white, an exchange of wedding rings, a kiss to seal their commitment after being pronounced married, and wedding cake served to guests. But more and more couples are adding personal touches that reflect their personalities, their families, and their interests, or they are forgoing tradition altogether.

Have Fun with Alternatives; Create Your Own Traditions

Destination weddings are popular these days. Couples who love the ocean might get married barefoot on the beach or hikers might get married high on a mountain.

People from different cultures may incorporate rituals and traditions to represent a union of the two different families. People with children from previous relationships often involve the young ones in the ceremony by inviting them to have special roles.

Instead of bridesmaids, consider a flurry of children to accompany the bride down the aisle like when Meghan Markle married Prince Harry.

In addition to taking passages from religious texts, read a favorite poem, short story, or quote about love and marriage. Anything goes, from Khalil Gibran to David Whyte, and Shel Silverstein to Dr. Seuss.

Writing wedding vows can infuse ritual with deeper meaning than standard cookie-cutter vows. We wrote ours with the help of the book *I Do! I Do!* My favorite line is still "I'll celebrate you when you're strong and cradle you when you're weak." We both had tears streaming down our faces when we said this to one another.

Wedding Rituals Around the World

In the Jewish tradition, after the rabbi pronounces the newlyweds, the couple smashes a glass in remembrance of the Temple of Jerusalem's destruction. It is also considered to symbolize that marriage is delicate and should be cared for and cherished.[12]

Quaker-style weddings involve a period of silent worship. After the couple says their vows, those in attendance may stand up to speak as they are so moved to share some words of inspiration for the couple or to read a quote or poem aloud.[13]

A wedding lasso made from an oversized rosary or a garland of flowers is a popular unity tradition in Catholic Latino and Filipino weddings. The lasso is placed in a figure eight around the couple while the priest blesses their marriage, symbolizing their union in the eyes of God.[14]

The Yoruba in West Africa have a wedding tradition called the tasting of the four elements to represent the many flavors of a marriage. A couple will eat a lemon or lime to represent the sourness they will face, sip vinegar to represent the bitterness they will encounter, take a pinch of cayenne pepper to signify the spice and passion they can bring into the relationship, and finally, they'll enjoy a spoonful of honey to represent the sweetness they can experience in marriage.[15]

Here are some considerations for personalizing weddings:

- **Be sure to include the personalities of the two people getting married.** When my friends Eileen and Lars got married, they played music from Jersey rocker Bon Jovi and country star Alan Jackson at their wedding ceremony to represent their union of North and South, at the same time showcasing their playfulness.

- **Stress the importance of the commitment to the family being created.** Ashley Mitchell shared, "I had a son from my first marriage. He was three when I remarried. The way the wedding venue was designed, the bride walked downstairs first, then down the aisle. I walked down the stairs by myself, and my dad met me at the bottom. He hugged me and kissed me and then handed my son's hand to me. My son and I walked down the aisle together as we would be a package entering into this new marriage."

- **Involve family and friends in the wedding celebrations.** Michelle and Jim Franco entered their union by inviting all of their friends and family to participate in their special day which was celebrated in Bend, Oregon. They sent out invitations that said "This will be a cocreated experience in our backyard. We would love for you to bring whatever you can to contribute to our special day." As a result, their family and friends contributed in the ways that felt best for them. Some brought poetry or readings for the ceremony. Others prepared food or brought flowers. Michelle's brother brought a magnificent wedding cake. Michelle admitted that she liked to be surprised so in true potluck style, the couple didn't know what people would be bringing until the actual day of the ceremony.

- **Invite heritage into the ceremony**. Judy Schneider of Abiquiu, New Mexico married a man of Cherokee lineage who had a nine-year-old son. As people entered the wedding circle in the middle of a powwow, his son was dressed in regalia and offered a smudge of sage to all who chose to enter the ceremony.

- **Use nature as the venue.** When Betsy and Jennifer got married during sunset at the beach on Anna Maria Island in

Florida, all eyes were on the beautiful brides and the sky's spectacular hues of orange, yellow, pink, and purple. Seagulls flew overhead as the waves lapped the shoreline. It was a stunning scene, and everyone was fully engaged in the moment and the magic that was occurring in front of them as the couple said, "I do."

- **Honor ancestors.** Wearing a dress or veil, carrying an embroidered handkerchief, or adorning some heirloom jewelry that belonged to a mother, grandmother, or other relative is a wonderful way for women to honor their ancestry. Men may choose to carry a pocket watch or wear a piece of jewelry that was passed down from a father, grandfather, or another male relative. A photo gallery or a slideshow of the couple could include images of family members and also showcase images of ancestors. In some Black or African weddings, there is a *libation* ceremony which is a ritual pouring of a liquid (this could be wine, liquor, or water) as both an invitation and an offering for the ancestors and gods to be present at the event.[16]

Personalizing the Rehearsal Dinner

It's not just the wedding ceremony itself that needs attention, but also the events related to the wedding celebration.

Licia and Peter Berry were married in a simple affair with just the two of them and a justice of the peace when they were in their early twenties. So, when it was time to help their eldest son, Jess, marry his high school sweetheart in a larger, more elaborate celebration than their own, they weren't quite sure what to do. They felt overwhelmed and a little unsure about how to move forward with their role in the wedding planning.

Licia confided, "I am an earth-based goddess-y shamanic practitioner and we have never done anything traditionally. When our boys were young, in a matter of two months, we effectively gave up the American dream. We quit our jobs, sold our home, pulled our kids out of school, bought an RV, and traveled around the country for two and a half years together. Jess and his brother had a very unconventional growing up."

I invited them to consider that the night before the wedding, traditionally the rehearsal dinner, was their opportunity to reflect on their side of the family. The Berrys consider themselves to be fun, eclectic, funky, hippie, woo-woo, and free-spirited, and I encouraged them to embrace that.

As we brainstormed together, it became clear that they wanted to create something unique and lots of fun, something that Jess and Tori and their friends would really appreciate. The end result turned out beautifully and accurately represented the joy-filled and fun-loving side of their family. I know this firsthand because I was also a guest at the wedding, having known Jess since he was a boy. Here are the highlights:

- They rented the Challenger Space Center in Tallahassee. Peter painstakingly created a twenty-minute video montage of photos featuring Jess and Tori growing up which was shown on the big IMAX screen during cocktails and appetizers.

- They decorated the party space with colorful banners, multicolored lanterns with twinkling lights inside, cactus stencils on the tablecloths, and blankets on the tables to reflect Jess's southwestern heritage since he was born in Arizona and identifies more with that part of the country, despite now living on the East Coast.

- They served a wide variety of food to reflect the family's love of ethnic cuisine. There were Mexican street tacos, Mediterranean stuffed grape leaves and goulash, Asian spicy shrimp, dumplings, and more.

- The groom's cake reflected Jess's profession as an audio engineer and was complete with a very detailed and completely edible sub-woofer and all the tools of his trade, including pliers and screws.

- When Peter and Licia gave a toast to Jess and Tori, they made reference to the fact that "we're a little odd" and a roar went up from the crowd. Jess and Tori's friends adored the fact that their family was creative, zany, and a little different, and it was well received by their peer group.

This is a great example of understanding celebration style. Licia and Peter are definitely not traditionalists and in this particular instance, wanted to be creative enthusiasts to celebrate the union of these two young people. When we can get in touch with how we want to honor and recognize a special occasion in our lives and not feel like we have to do what is expected or fit into the norm, we can get as playful as we like and create a more authentic experience for all.

Wedding Anniversaries

I remember attending a women's retreat with Helene Van Manen, a coach in Beulah, Colorado in 2008. I was enamored of her love story with her sweet husband Dave as they had driven out of New York City in a Volkswagen van when they were teenagers and headed west, never to look back! I asked the secret to their success with thirty years of marriage (at the time) under their belts. Her reply was "Oh, Elizabeth, I do believe we've had eight distinct marriages in those thirty years!" Her response has stayed with me all these years as a reminder that as we grow and evolve, so do our primary relationships.

Rituals to celebrate wedding anniversaries are important to mark the passage of time and the distinct chapters that a couple may go through together. A five-year wedding anniversary celebration is likely to look a lot different from a fifty-year celebration. Some couples, on their anniversary, return to the restaurant or outdoor spot where they got engaged. They might eat the same food or drink the same wine. Every time Eric and I eat goat cheese-stuffed and bacon-wrapped dates, we reminisce about how delicious they were at our wedding!

Couples who have been married for decades may have more time and resources to plan a special trip to commemorate the occasion. Dave and Kathy Ness from Rochester, Minnesota planned a trip to Scandinavia with their two adult daughters so they could have quality time with just the four of them (no spouses or grandkids on this particular trip). They had been doing genealogical research on their family tree and went over to meet relatives they had recently discovered for the very first time. It was a special family bonding time.

A Canadian friend of mine has incredibly generous grandparents who treated their entire family to an eleven-day Caribbean cruise to the ABC Islands (Aruba, Bonaire, and Curaçao) to celebrate their sixtieth wedding anniversary—twenty-five people in total, including children, spouses, grandchildren, and even one great-grandchild! In our modern society with relatives who live geographically distanced from one another, it is a rare treat for extended family members to all be together and share meals, love, and laughter for an extended time.

But it isn't necessary to spend lots of money or go on a trip to create a memorable ritual to celebrate love. During 2020 and the COVID restrictions when everyone was staying home as much as possible, I remember reading about a couple whose children learned the meal they ate on their wedding day and then did their best to recreate that culinary experience at home. They decorated the dining room by setting the table with linen, using fine china, lighting candles, and they invited their parents to dress up for their special anniversary meal.

Whatever you do, whether it is a simple exchange of cards and gifts or an elaborate week-long trip, be sure to do something to honor your special day. Anniversaries of all kinds are important, but honoring the day you said "I do" is deserving of your presence and attention, especially in the fast-paced busy world we live in.

Chapter Ten
Moving

I have moved twelve times in thirty years (technically eighteen including the same-city moves, but who's counting?), and I think it is fair to say that I am an expert at it. I have learned how to buy and sell homes and how to declutter my belongings to only move the essentials, and I have developed the art of saying goodbye to my community, and then saying hello as I settle in to make new friends.

Is it easy? Not at all. It is stressful, exhausting, and overwhelming, especially when there are children and pets involved—it is much easier to move as a single person, but even that is not simple. Moving involves tremendous physical, mental, and emotional stamina, and I have been reduced to tears at least once on every single move I have ever made. Whether it is saying goodbye to friends, leaving a home that is loved, or the uncertainty of what lies ahead, stepping out of the comfort zone into unfamiliar territory can be daunting.

But is it rewarding? In most cases, it absolutely can be. Relocating for a new job, a new relationship, or simply for a change of pace can evoke joy, excitement, and opportunity. Living in a new home can spark creativity, relationships, and a new way of being. Living in a new city, state, or country can introduce the opportunity to meet people, see places, and enjoy experiences that will broaden horizons and can potentially change the trajectory of life.

That certainly happened for me. I committed to my coaching business full time, and I met my husband after moving to North Carolina, and we adopted our daughter after moving to Florida.

I've moved for the reasons that many of us do—to go to school, to get married, to start a new job, and for family connections. Occasionally, a move is simply across town, and other times it is being transplanted to a completely new country. Some people move regularly for their jobs (think military personnel) and get good at it. Others may only move once or twice in a lifetime, and find it to be very traumatic for them, making such a big change after a lifetime in one place. Joyful reasons make it emotionally easier to relocate, but sometimes people have to move under challenging circumstances as the result of divorce, death, or foreclosure. In those situations, it is especially important to ask for help from friends and seek emotional support to navigate the transition.

No matter why someone is moving, it is a major transition that can be filled with a complicated mix of upheaval, letting go, excitement, and possibility. It can render us swollen with grief or infuse us with hope for the future—in some cases, a little of both. Regardless of the circumstances, there are always challenges to be overcome and gifts to be recognized and received.

Because I am an "experienced relocator," I have had good moves and bad ones. One of the key elements in creating what I consider to be a successful move is to make sure to properly say goodbye when leaving one place, and then to properly say hello when beginning a new chapter. Saying goodbye to the physical

Chapter Ten: Moving

space of a home and land is just as important as saying goodbye to the community of friends and neighbors. Designing rituals as containers to allow that exchange is critical to a smooth transition.

Proper goodbyes are about completion. They are about bringing things full circle and honoring the life cycle of an experience. They are about recognizing and appreciating all aspects of a chapter in our lives. Goodbyes are an opportunity to say thank you for all the learning and accomplishments and a chance to grieve any losses or heartaches that occurred during that time.

We see examples of goodbyes in many aspects of our daily lives. Business meetings are often closed with a summary of the meeting, a review of the action steps, and a thank you to everyone for participating. A well-written letter has an engaging opening, a comprehensive middle, and a summary statement with a closing salutation. A play at the theater has a powerful ending scene. Then, when the curtain closes, the actors come back on stage for a final bow. At a music concert, after the final applause, the performer may come back for one final song if the audience yells *Encore!* loud enough.

So, it makes sense, then, that a move should also include a beginning, a middle, and an end.

In 2001, after my first husband asked me for a divorce, I relocated to the beautiful mountains of Asheville, North Carolina. My best friend from high school lived there with her husband and infant daughter, and they encouraged me to come to the healing lands in western North Carolina. When I arrived, I rented a condo on top of a mountain surrounded by hilltops, that looked over the twinkling lights of the city at night, and I thought I had found my forever home. I felt I belonged in the majestic Blue Ridges—they had summoned me there and by heeding the call, I would be rewarded by getting to stay there for eternity. I was tired of moving and craved a place to land permanently.

But life had different plans for me. I fell in love again a few years later with Eric, and we married in 2004. My three kitties and I moved from my mountaintop tree house-like condo into his 1950s bachelor pad ranch with Eric and Andy the dog. Talk about an adjustment for all of us!

We learned a year later that the BASF manufacturing plant where he worked would eventually be shutting down. He had been with the German chemical giant his entire career and in order to stay employed with them, he would need to accept a transfer to Florida.

While I didn't want to leave Asheville, I understood this was important for his career and because my work is easily mobile, I agreed to move. I have a lot of relatives in Florida, so it was appealing to live closer to them for a few years. He interviewed for several positions within the company, and in the summer of 2007, we packed up our things and our four furry friends and relocated to the oak-lined streets of Tallahassee.

Let me be clear. I really did not want to move. I loved the mountains and the climate. I loved my friends. I loved my life there. But ultimately, I loved my husband more.

I remember standing in my kitchen with my book club girlfriends gathered around, and I completely broke down into tears. They started crying with me saying things like, "We don't want you to go."

I was sad for several months leading up to our departure. But another friend offered a different perspective, "Elizabeth, your time in Asheville is done. You came here to do what you needed to. And to learn what you needed to. And now Tallahassee needs you. That's why you are being called there."

I didn't really believe it at the time, but after a few years in Tallahassee, I could see what she suggested was true. And, as you read about the miracle arrival of our daughter, you understand that we needed to be in Tallahassee for the stars to align for that divine union.

To celebrate the amazing friendships that we had formed during our time in Asheville (sixteen years for Eric, six for me), we threw a massive goodbye party and invited our friends from work, volunteering, church, and our social circle. We rented a downtown restaurant owned by one of my coaching clients with a front row view of the skyline and the sparkling Fourth of July fireworks.

We chose a Florida theme, complete with typical Sunshine State foods and drinks, and we hosted a costume contest. We dubbed a winner for the "Mr. and Mrs. Sunshine" award, and it happened to be two friends of ours who were dating, and subsequently got married the next year. She was dressed as a tacky tourist complete with a Hawaiian shirt, zinc oxide on her nose, floppy hat, sunglasses, and a camera around her neck—back in the days before we had cameras on our phones. He wore only shorts and had painted his body from head to toe, half royal blue and the other half bright orange—the colors of the University of Florida Gators.

When we gathered everyone around to present the award, we took a few minutes to give a toast of gratitude to all our friends. We told them how much they meant to us and how much we would miss them. We extended the invitation for each of them to visit us at any time. We had so many fond memories of fun parties, and we recounted them with glee.

Soon after, just a week before our actual move, our dear friend Mista Whitson hosted a very intimate gathering of our closest friends at her home. She went all out with preparing our favorite foods, baking delicious desserts, and decorating her home with beautiful flowers and twinkling lights. It was a very elegant evening, and she invited our friends to take turns giving us blessings and good wishes as we prepared to leave Asheville and begin our new life in Tallahassee. It was such a lovely gift from the heart, and we cried many tears that night as we felt loved and appreciated by so many dear friends.

Fast forward a year. We had left North Carolina in 2007 thinking our house was sold. However, the contract blew up because we had a buried oil tank and discovered that we had contaminated soil on our lot. Finally, after a year of remediation and struggling with the state to work out all the details, we sold our house.

When we returned in the summer of 2008 to say goodbye for good, we gathered at the empty house and invited our friends to bring over beer for one last get-together that felt much more like a ritual than our trademark parties. We sat around on the empty kitchen counters and recalled all of the fun gatherings that we had hosted in that house for many years, oftentimes staying up until 4 a.m. dancing the night away through wedding showers, Christmas gatherings, New Year's Eve celebrations, dinner parties, and book club get-togethers. It was an impromptu but very sweet final, *final* hurrah with our friends, and one that also allowed us to truly let go of that space.

Those are just a few personal stories from one exceptionally significant move in my life, but there are many ways to say goodbye, and hello, with meaning and intention. The key is to personalize the experiences of relocation in a way that resonates with all involved.

Make a plan, or several, to say goodbye to the people that matter most. If a friend offers to throw a going away party, it might be wise to gratefully accept this generous gift. Sometimes it can be difficult to throw a goodbye party for yourself so if there are generous friends who offer, take them up on it.

Or, if you like throwing parties like me, plan a gathering at your home, a favorite restaurant, or a favorite spot in nature where you invite your friends to go hiking or have a picnic at the park. Planning one big gathering can be logistically easier, or you may want to consider doing smaller get-togethers with several groups of friends—a cookout with neighbors, a business lunch with professional colleagues, a potluck with church friends, and so on. It doesn't really matter what you do, what matters is that you take time for specific closure and concrete goodbyes.

While it may evoke hefty emotions, allow yourself to really feel them. Let people tell you how much you mean to them and how much they will miss you. Say those words to your friends so they know how much they mean to you. You may shed a lot of tears, but your friends will be grateful for the open-hearted exchange when you have moved on to your new life in your new city.

When I moved away from my beloved Asheville, North Carolina, my book club created an entire scrapbook for me. They each took two pages and included their favorite photographs, recounted silly stories, and wrote love notes about how much they appreciated our friendship. I adored it when they gave it to me, but it was months later, sitting on the floor of my new home office in Florida when I pulled out the album, that I cried buckets of tears.

At that point, I had not yet established myself in the community and was lonely and depressed. Reading through those pages, reliving the fun parties and playful times we had shared, gave me hope that I could once again create community and surround myself with amazing women.

Say a proper goodbye to your house with a *moving out* ritual. In our Western, modernized culture, we tend to think of a house as simply a place to live. But many ancient traditions believe that the home is an extension of your body, your spirit, and your family. The Chinese have practiced feng shui for 5000+ years and teach that there is both an art and a science to help harmonize with your surrounding environment, including both home and land.

Denise Linn, author of *Sacred Space*, writes, "Our homes are mirrors of ourselves. They reflect our interests, our beliefs, our hesitations, our spirit, and our passion. They tell a story about how we feel about ourselves and the world around us. Home is more than a place to lay your head and seek comfort from the elements. And it is a place where you can interface with the universe."[17]

Whether you have lived in your home, apartment, or condominium for one year or thirty, consider doing a house blessing to express gratitude—to say goodbye as you prepare to release your home and make way for a new owner or steward of the space. Customize it to match your needs, whether you are single, partnered, or have a family.

Here are some sensory elements to incorporate into a house blessing ceremony:

- **Candles**—Fire is pure energy and is often used in ceremonies to help us feel connected to Spirit. Burn candles to help purify and transform space, and to set positive intentions for what lies ahead.

- **Incense or plants**—Smoke has long been used for metaphysical cleansing in ancient traditions around the world. Burning incense is a great way to clear a space of negative energies—some popular choices are sandalwood, frankincense, and myrrh. Burning herbs like rosemary, cedar, or mugwort is also recommended.

    It is important to note burning sage and smudging has been popularized in the West, but it is an Indigenous American practice, and non-Indigenous people burning sage is considered cultural appropriation and disrespectful: the unethical and unsustainable practices for harvesting sage should also be considered. Research the traditions of your own lineage to find what feels good to you.

- **Salt**—Throwing salt to support the purification, protection, and blessing of a home and its inhabitants has been used in diverse cultures and can usually be found in any pantry.

Chapter Ten: Moving

- **Sound**—Using bells, cymbals, or drums are a great way to create sound to purify, protect, and bless a home. If those aren't available, clapping of hands or singing songs work nicely, especially if children are involved. Choose songs that are meaningful to the children to keep them engaged.

Try writing a letter to the home thanking it for all of the lessons and experiences that were experienced there. It can be read aloud, then burned in a fire pit in the backyard. Another idea is to write a letter to the new stewards of the home and leave it for them on the counter, letting them know how much the home was appreciated and how blessings and best wishes are offered to them now that they are the new owners.

A "house cooling party" which is a term in the Urban Dictionary for a goodbye party, is a fun and festive gathering different from a more sacred goodbye ritual. It is the opposite of a housewarming, where you gather your friends (like Eric and I did when we left Asheville) to tell stories and recount favorite times in the home together. A fun twist on the housewarming party is that instead of people bringing gifts, you give guests gifts in the form of items that won't be moving with you. Leave them out and invite friends to depart with a treasured token or memento that once belonged to you.

Say a proper hello to your new home with a house blessing ceremony. It can be very exciting to move into a new space and start fresh. But it also can be overwhelming. It is easy to get caught up in the details of placing furniture and unpacking boxes. A house blessing is a lovely way to fully integrate into a new home with meaning and intention.

The first product that I created in the Sacred Celebrations gift line is a house blessing ritual kit with a spray made from essential oils, a clear quartz crystal, a warm vanilla candle, and a rosemary bundle. The kit has become a bestseller, and homeowners love the experiential nature of the gift complete with instructions to help design their own ritual.

Tracy Weber, an equine and educational consultant in Frankenmuth, Michigan, got married and moved into the home that her husband and his ex-wife built. She did a few house-clearing rituals, including smoke cleansing and placing crystals in specific places in the home, to help shift the energy, all the while setting intentions to infuse the home with love.

She laughed as she recounted this story to me, "One thing I did was open the front and back doors. In the middle of winter. In Michigan. At the Rotary club meeting that week, a friend told me that he drove by and wondered what the heck was going on… I explained I was ridding the house of negative energy—he laughed and said he understood. Now I'm so grateful we've created a happy home!"

Many religions also have house blessing ceremonies. In some Christian traditions, a house is blessed by a priest or minister who walks through the home sprinkling holy water and saying prayers, asking God to watch over the people living in the house. In the Hindu tradition, a *puja* (ritual ceremony) is performed to bless a new house. It usually involves a *pundit* (Hindu priest) leading the participants in mantras and in songs and can include ritual elements like banging a gong, blowing a conch shell, walking through each room of the house with a lamp or fire, and making bountiful food offerings to the gods.

A Buddhist house blessing is facilitated by a group of monks and involves sacred water, wax candles, and chanting over white holy thread, which is then tied onto the wrists of the home's inhabitants. Family and friends are invited to the ceremony, and after the monks have been fed and properly thanked with gifts, the remaining guests sit down to a celebration feast.[18] Habitat for Humanity, a global non-profit housing organization, offers a dedication ceremony and house blessing for every new home that it builds. All the volunteers who helped build the home are invited back and it is a joyful celebration of the new homeowners.[19]

Carlton Brown, an Atlanta-based chef and entrepreneur, grew up attending the Baptist church where he was raised in Jacksonville, North Carolina. He recalls that his grandparents were deeply religious and said, "My grandmother was always praying. I believe a lot of the blessings I have received in my life have to do with my grandmother's prayers." Every New Year's Day, he remembers their pastor from church would arrive early in the morning and walk around the house with intention and speak aloud prayers and blessings for their home and for their family. This happened every year, so he didn't regard this practice as unique or special, it was just a part of normal life.

Performing a house blessing doesn't have to be religious and can happen at any time that you deem necessary or helpful. Here are a few ideal times to design a house blessing ritual.

- **Moving into a new home.** Establish a positive relationship with the house and the land that is new to you and your family.

- **Beginning of a new year.** Freshen the energy and set inspiring intentions for the new year.

- **Change in the household.** Perhaps someone has moved in or moved out, a loved one has died, or there's been a renovation to the space that created chaos and is ready to be rebalanced.

- **The house feels stagnant.** Sometimes the energy in your home simply feels stuck and you can't necessarily figure out why.

- **On a regular basis.** Every month on the new moon which represents new beginnings, the first of the month, or at the change of seasons.

Chapter Eleven
Divorce

Divorce sucks. Quite simply, it is one of the most painful experiences a person can go through, regardless of the circumstances, who initiated it, and whether it is a quickie divorce or drags out for years. The Holmes and Rahe Stress Scale, a psychological instrument that ranks the most stressful major life events that people endure, lists divorce as second only behind the death of the spouse.[20]

That makes sense because divorce *is* the death we don't acknowledge in our society. When someone dies, we hold funerals and celebrations of life. We remember the person, we celebrate their contributions, we recount stories, and we cherish precious memories. But with divorce, which is often equally painful, we simply move forward instead of taking time to pause and honor the gifts, learning experiences, and outcomes (sometimes children) of that union. The American Psychological Association states that between 40 and 50 percent of marriages end in divorce which means that a lot of us are in need of ways to manage our grief during this painful transition.[21]

Divorce is the death of a marriage, the death of a family, the death of friendships, the death of safety, the death of support, and the death of life as a person knows it. But in Debbie Ford's book *Spiritual Divorce*, she teaches that divorce can actually be a catalyst for an extraordinary life if a person is open to the spiritual wake-up call that it provides. This book was a lifesaver for me when I went through my divorce years ago.

My Divorce Story

I met my first husband in English class during my junior year of high school in Ridgefield, Connecticut. I had gotten in trouble for talking at the back of the class, so Mrs. Rhodes put me in the front seat of the front row against the wall. If I made a subtle quarter turn in my chair, I could sit with my back against the wall and clandestinely write notes to Dirk, who sat directly behind me.

I knew intuitively at the age of sixteen that I would eventually marry and spend my life with him. We went to senior prom together and had an on-again-off-again long-distance relationship during college and his stint in the military. Soon after my father died and he was deployed to Iraq and then returned safely home, he asked me, in front of the Christmas tree, to marry him. I was twenty-five when we married in 1995, and I thought we would live happily ever after.

He asked me for a divorce five and a half years into our marriage. By telephone. We were in the middle of moving from Philadelphia to Seattle and he moved a few months ahead of me to start his new job while I stayed behind to complete my work commitments and sell our house. We had been having problems for about a year and had gone to several counseling sessions together.

A few weeks into this physical separation, he realized he was done, and when he called me in April of 2001, he told me not to come—not to move to Seattle with him. He couldn't even say the word *divorce* until I insisted.

Chapter Eleven: Divorce

I refused to believe it was true until he flew home cross country and looked me in the eye. I fell sobbing into his arms when I realized he was serious. We spent the weekend together, sorting through our things, determining who would keep what. It was all very agreeable and also surreal. That last painful night in our home, I remember saying goodnight to him. He headed upstairs to sleep in the guest room, and I was a puddle on the white linoleum kitchen floor. I wailed and sobbed and gasped for breath so loudly that he heard me from upstairs and came back down to hold me as I rocked, my body filled with anguish and despair.

After he left, I remember being so sick that I had laryngitis for days. I walked around our home and ripped all our gorgeous pieces from the walls. Our favorite thing to do was travel and we had bought local artwork on our trips together. I could no longer stand to look at them.

I remember being so angry that I picked up the telephone (back before cell phones, when they were heavy) and hurled it across the living room where it made a significant dent in the wall. I just wanted to break things, the way *he* had broken our marriage. I experienced a depth of rage that I'd never before imagined possible.

I have not seen him since the day he walked out of our house for good.

It took almost a year and a half for the divorce to be finalized because we both moved out of state from where we had been living. That was the time I relocated to the sacred mountains of Asheville, North Carolina.

I arrived shell-shocked and shattered into a million pieces. There were days when I could barely leave my apartment, but I forced myself to go to the grocery store to buy milk just so that I could talk with the cashier. I did not work for three months. I lived off my meager savings and cried and raged daily. I met with a therapist and spiritual counselor who encouraged me to write an "anger letter," which to this day, is one of the most effective tools

I have found for expressing my authentic self. Let me tell you, that letter was long.

People going through a painful breakup look for relief anywhere they can get it, often turning to alcohol, drugs, sex, gambling, or shopping.

While I definitely overindulged with drinking at get-togethers, I also went for long hikes in the mountains and soaked in the beauty of Mother Nature. I started taking yoga classes and I discovered Nia—a fusion of dance, martial arts, and mindfulness. I worked hard to shift the anxiety, worry, and fears I was experiencing by getting out of my head and back into my body. I read books by spiritual teachers like Louise Hay, Julia Cameron, and don Miguel Ruiz. I believe that year was really the beginning of my spiritual awakening, or as author, professor, and speaker Brené Brown calls it, my spiritual breakdown, *er, breakthrough.*

During this time, I made friends with a wise woman named Pam, a realtor and feng shui consultant, who suggested that I consider doing a divorce ritual once everything was finalized. She had been divorced twice but was a happy, sparkly person full of *joie de vivre*, so I figured she knew what she was talking about.

At the time, I hadn't consciously designed my own ritual before, but I understood that a ritual was a sacred ceremony to help support life's big passages. I remember helping my mom plan my father's funeral, and Dirk and I had planned a beautiful wedding ceremony, but this was the first time I had created a ritual just for me. The idea of taking a series of deliberate actions to help me process the death of my marriage and death of my life as I had known it was very appealing.

The first ritual was simple and spontaneous. The day I was served with divorce papers felt like a shock to the system. I immediately sent out an email to my friends and asked them to join me for pizza and beer that evening while they witnessed me signing the papers. I was amazed that over a dozen friends showed up on such short notice. Several of them had been divorced already, so they understood my pain. Their show of solidarity buoyed my spirits during such a heartbreaking time. They were beacons of hope to let me know that not only would I survive, but one day I would again thrive.

Dirk was in Seattle, Washington the actual day of our divorce, and I was on the East Coast in Asheville. He was going to the courthouse that day and promised to call me as soon as everything was finalized. I had done some preparation and knew that it would be a pivotal turning point in my life. I started the day by taking off my wedding ring. While I had not been wearing it since the separation, I put it on one last time the night before the divorce.

I then dug my tennis racket out of the closet and proceeded to beat the hell out of every single piece of furniture in my house. I beat my queen-sized bed. I beat my couch. I beat my loveseat. I beat my oversized gorgeously upholstered crimson and gold Ethan Allen chairs. It was all once ours and I reasoned that this was a safe and healthy way to express my rage without breaking anything or requiring me to go purchase new furniture which I could not afford. Releasing my frustrations and sending my perceived negativity into the furniture helped me to shift an association from we to me.

Fortunately for my kitty cats, that part of the ritual didn't last too long and after cowering in the laundry room for a while, when things got quieter, they eventually poked their heads out to see what I was doing next.

I proceeded to move through my condo one room at a time and I lit a ceremonial fire in each. There is something deeply primal and oh-so-powerful about fire as a tool for transformation. Using a large Pyrex bowl, I put in a little bit of Epsom salts and rubbing alcohol, and then I lit a match. I had a bowl of water nearby in case the fire got out of hand. With each tiny fire, I forcefully spoke out loud the things that I was ready to release from my marriage. After I completed that sequence, I went back through each room in the house and instead lit a tealight candle. For each candle that sparked, I calmly and intentionally claimed all the things I desired in this new chapter of my life.

After doing all that energy clearing, I was ravenous. I stopped and ate lunch and grounded myself with healthy and nurturing food. That afternoon, I spent time relocating twenty-seven items in my home. It is a feng shui strategy for helping to shift the energy in any space. So, I moved furniture, hung artwork, and got rid of clutter. That took me most of the afternoon.

In the evening, I invited three of my closest girlfriends to come over. I asked them to please bring me things that would help me to feel loved, nurtured, and supported. The four of us sat outside on my deck, surrounded by lush green trees and the setting sun.

One friend wrote me a lovely letter outlining my positive qualities and highlighting my courage. She assured me that all would be well. Another friend brought me a plant and a stunning collection of poems and inspirational quotes to lift me up. The third brought a "single woman survival kit" which included everything from lipstick to movie tickets to condoms! Laughter is truly the best medicine.

While they were there, Dirk called to tell me that he was no longer my husband. It was a terribly sad and lovingly sweet conversation. I had sent him some questions ahead of time via email that I wanted us to discuss together. While he was reluctant at first, I think he understood the value in having real closure.

The questions I asked him were:
- What did you learn about yourself during our marriage?
- What are your happiest memories of our fun times together?
- What do you wish for me and my future?

Lest you think that our divorce was agreeable, it was not. We fought a lot and the trauma of the breakup brought out the worst in both of us. So, as we closed our life chapter together, I wanted to make sure that our final connection was meaningful and honored the fifteen years of our relationship. We laughed and cried as we remembered silly things about our pets, the fun adventures we had experienced during our travels, and the losses we had endured as a family.

I thanked him for encouraging me to start my own business. Two decades later, he still gets the credit for being my number one cheerleader to become an entrepreneur.

I went to bed that night feeling exhausted and empty, but in a good way, like an empty vessel. I had ridden the roller coaster of emotions all day but ended the night feeling satisfied that I had done our death—the death of our marriage—honor and justice.

The next morning, I woke feeling fresh, new, and alive. A few days prior, I had purchased a new ring at a local boutique. I didn't have a lot of money at the time so replacing my diamond engagement ring with something expensive wasn't an option, but this shiny silver ring with a large round amethyst in the middle caught my eye and I knew I had to have it. I slipped it onto my ring finger as I committed from that day forward to be married to myself, to always love myself, to be committed to my best interests, and to never settle.

The third and final ritual involved a big party. Our divorce was final the last week of June, so I hosted a huge July 4th party at my condo and invited all my friends. It was my personal Independence Day party.

I lived on top of a mountain and just a little way down the road, there was an unobstructed view of the fireworks over the city of Asheville skyline. It was simply magical watching the brilliant fireworks light up the sky with a 360-degree view of the mountains in the background.

We had great food, delicious drinks, and plenty of music to dance to. My friends were so supportive, and they really celebrated the possibilities for me as a single woman. I remember looking around my condo and marveling at the incredible community that I had formed in barely a year's time. My girlfriends were huggy, my men friends were flirty, and I ended up kissing a handsome guy at the end of the evening, which made me feel sexy and alive.

Just four weeks later, I met the man who would become my second husband and father to our daughter.

I believe that I would not have been ready to be open to love again had I not done all the rituals surrounding my divorce.

Divorce Rituals

Divorce is tricky. There are messy divorces and there are mutually agreed upon divorces. Some involve intense amounts of heartache and heartbreak, and others involve a gradual separating of ways that is neither jarring nor dramatic. Some people maintain a healthy connection—even friendship—that can last a lifetime. Others never speak to one another or have any kind of contact ever again. It can prove especially challenging for people who have children together. They have to determine a new normal and do their best to make decisions in the best interest of the children while at the same time, taking care of their own emotional needs. Divorce impacts not just the two people in the marriage, but children, grandchildren, parents, siblings, and other extended family members.

Whenever people go through divorce, I always recommend therapy, spiritual direction, or some kind of outside counsel. It can be incredibly valuable to have the perspective of a third party to help one or both partners, mindfully disengage from the relationship. Just as couples go to premarital counseling or attend relationship workshops when they are preparing to commit to marriage, unraveling a committed relationship deserves the same amount of care and attention to fully process it.

Divorce is not just an ending. It is a beginning as well. Just as we mark the death of a loved one with a memorial service, some kind of divorce ritual, divorce ceremony, or marriage dissolution event can help both parties, and the people who love them (especially children that are a product of the marriage) to honor the marriage for what it was and also help look forward to the future. It can be an energetic shift from we to me again, just like I experienced during my own beating of the furniture, which is incredibly helpful and freeing as people move forward into the next chapter of their lives.

"A marriage begins with ritual and ceremony, and it should end that way," says Risa Marlen, a marriage and family therapist in Teaneck, NJ, who has conducted divorce ceremonies and was quoted in an article in the *New York Times*. "The human psyche needs that closure. It warrants it. It deserves it."[22]

Some religious traditions now offer divorce ceremonies for their congregants. The Unitarian Universalist Church offers a ceremony of hope. The Jewish faith offers a "get" (a divorce document) and a ceremony can be officiated by a rabbi. Several Christian churches—Methodist, Presbyterian, Lutheran, and Episcopal—offer divorce blessing ceremonies or special prayers.

There are other unique ways to mark the occasion as well. A documentary called *The Lovers: The Great Wall Walk* was made about a couple who decided to end their relationship with a ritual of walking the Great Wall in China. In 1988, they each started at a different end and walked for ninety days where they met in the middle, embraced, and said goodbye.[23]

In her book *The State of Affairs: Rethinking Infidelity*, relationship expert Esther Perel encourages couples to write goodbye letters to one another. Perel suggests that a person write a letter that is never actually given to the ex-partner. Or agree to write letters to one another and share them, potentially reading them aloud with the help of a trained therapist if it would help to process the emotions. She recommends things like recalling favorite memories, what each will miss about the partner, how they impacted each other's life positively, asking for forgiveness, expressing anger, and more.[24] Expressing emotions in writing can be a powerfully cathartic experience both for the writer and the receiver.

Katherine Woodward Thomas, author of the book *Conscious Uncoupling* also teaches about the importance of breaking up a relationship with decency, honor, and respect. She encourages couples to work with a trained therapist, but it is written so one may also work through the steps alone.

The five steps are as follows:

1. Find emotional freedom.
2. Reclaim your power and your life.
3. Break the pattern, heal your heart.
4. Become a love alchemist.
5. Reinvent your life.

Taking time to invest in the process of inner reflection and intentional dialogue is a ritual in and of itself where the two people separating can say what needs to be said, experience a wide range of feelings, and then each make a plan to move forward with their lives as individuals.[25]

Here are three examples of divorces with different circumstances that might suggest different rituals to process the emotions and the experience:

After twenty years of marriage, Carrie's husband had an affair with his secretary and remarried within a year of their divorce. They share custody of their daughter, but it is still incredibly painful several years later.

This ritual might focus on grief and loss and create a sacred ceremony to honor the deep and complex emotions involved with letting go of one's hopes and dreams. With the support of loving friends, Carrie could start by burning pieces of paper where she writes out her anger, resentment, and fear and asks for those emotions to be cleared away. Then, releasing white roses or carnations into a body of water and speaking aloud her grief and feelings of loss and asking for gentleness and ease in the days ahead, could help to support her in the new chapter of her life as a single mom.

Steve and his wife divorced after ten years of friendship and seven years of marriage, no kids. But he has been part of the family for almost two decades, so he is still invited to celebrate Thanksgiving and Christmas with his ex-wife's family. He even lives next door to his former sister-in-law, who is still one of his best friends.

When two people simply grow apart, a ritual can really honor what the individuals learned from one another and focus on their newfound freedoms and opportunities for the new life that lies ahead. They could write letters to one another or have an intentional conversation like I did with my ex-husband expressing what they learned from each other and what they wish for each other going forward.

After seventeen years, Melinda found the courage to leave her loveless marriage. She moved into a studio apartment and left her beautiful suburban home to her husband and daughter. Her ex-husband is the primary parent, and she spends time with her teenage daughter on weekends. They all still gather for holidays, and each parent brings their new partner. They are navigating the true definition of a modern family with as much grace as possible.

A ritual here might very intentionally involve the children. This can help to redefine the family unit and reaffirm to the children that while the parents may not continue to be married or even love one another, the love for their children will always be primary and paramount. In a private family gathering, parents could read aloud commitments to the children about continuing to love and care for them, and parents can make statements to one another in front of the children about continuing to co-parent with respect, love, and friendship.

Questions to Consider When Planning a Divorce Ritual:

1. What are the circumstances surrounding divorce? Did you choose to leave your partner? Did they choose to leave you? Was it mutual?

2. What are the emotions surrounding the divorce? Once you have identified the primary emotions, think about how you want to express or resolve them.

3. Who else is impacted by this divorce other than you and your partner? What might they need for closure, and do you want to invite them to be part of your ritual?

4. What kind of support do you want and need during this time of transition? Do you need space and quiet and time to cry? Do you need laughter and silliness and time with friends? Do you need time to talk one-on-one with your partner?

5. If you decide to have a one-on-one conversation with your partner as your divorce is finalized, what might you want to say to one another?

6. What are your happiest memories from the marriage?

7. What did you learn about yourself and the marriage?

8. What is your wish as you move forward into the next chapter of your lives?

Hope for the Future

On the popular blog Scary Mommy, contributor Julie Danielson wrote, "In the middle of my unraveling marriage, it never occurred to me that my life was going to be better because I had the courage to get a divorce."[26]

I would say that for the vast majority of divorced people I have met since my own divorce in 2002, this is a common sentiment. They talk about living more authentically and feeling freer to be themselves.

My client Ellie shared with me the following: "Twelve years ago was the worst day of my life. I was seven months pregnant with my second child and found out that my husband was having an affair with a twenty-two-year-old cocktail waitress. We divorced shortly afterward. For many years, I dreaded the anniversary of this discovery until I realized how far our family had come and evolved. Now I look at it as my own special day of victory. It's the day that I took my life into my own hands and decided to start living for myself. I now send myself a big bouquet of flowers every year with an anniversary card celebrating this very special day."

While divorce is incredibly painful, it's often one of the most powerful growth experiences someone will ever go through.

Chapter Twelve
Death and Loss

Grief is not reserved only for those closest to us. We may mourn the loss of a great leader, a wonderful humanitarian, or an artist who taught us how to appreciate beauty in profound ways. Perhaps one of the most famous funerals in modern history was that of Princess Diana in 1997. Her funeral parade was watched by two billion people around the world. If you ask people of a certain generation where they were on the day Princess Diana died, chances are they distinctly remember how and when they heard the news of her death. She was a beloved and revered person, and so many people wanted to pay their respects and process the loss of The People's Princess.

We may also need support in processing our collective grief, such as mourning the lives lost in the Indian Ocean tsunami in 2004 or the attack on the World Trade Center in New York City on September 11, 2001. Or we may have to process historical grief when learning about war, especially the millions of deaths in the Nazi concentration camps in Germany during World War II or the lives lost when the US dropped the atomic bombs on Hiroshima and Nagasaki in Japan.

We often hear pithy sayings such as "life is precious" or "time is short," but these reminders do not have much meaning until you experience the death of a loved one and it suddenly becomes personal. Some people make it into midlife before they experience any serious losses. Others have parents or siblings die when they are children, and their perspective on death is different since they had exposure to loss at such a tender age.

I remember talking with a friend after my mother passed away, and she commented that I was moving through the emotions of grieving so well.

My honest reply was, "Well, I've had a lot of experience with death."

It is true. I have experienced the loss of all of my grandparents, both parents, several aunts, uncles and cousins, seven pets, and the miscarriage of twin babies. In addition, I have had two friends, my next-door neighbor, a few clients die, and my best friend died when I was only six years old. So yeah, I guess I have had more exposure to death than some.

During those experiences, I have learned that the best way to process grief is not to avoid it or to sidestep it but to face it head-on. Giving myself permission to express my grief in tangible ways—crying, sleeping a lot, binge-watching television, withdrawing from social interaction for a period of time—allowed me to navigate each event and return to equilibrium faster than if I had stuffed the emotions and tried to plow through pretending everything was okay.

Whether or not you have had a lot of experience with death and loss, the fact remains that in our westernized culture, we don't seem well equipped to deal with it. For many reasons, our society is *death averse*. We have the false belief that perhaps if we don't talk about something, it will not make an appearance in our lives. At least not yet. But if we do not properly express our grief and allow for outlets to process the natural emotions that come when we experience a great loss, it can lead to sickness, depression, and other debilitating diseases. And even when we do take time to plan or attend a funeral, talk with loved ones about the person who has died, etc., we are still left grappling with some of life's biggest questions: *Why them? Why me? Why now?*

You may be familiar with Elisabeth Kübler-Ross's five stages of grief, which were first introduced in her groundbreaking book *On Death and Dying* in 1969. The stages are denial, anger, bargaining, depression, and acceptance. As her work evolved over time, she was clear to point out that not everyone experiences all of those stages and that they are not necessarily linear experiences. But using these emotions as a framework can help people understand and process any grief they may be experiencing.[27] When my mom was dying, I found great comfort in reading Kübler-Ross's book, coauthored with David Kessler, *On Grief and Grieving,* and Kessler's book *The Needs of the Dying*.

Planning and participating in death rituals are vital for the loved ones left behind. It is important to express the entire range of emotions because that is all part of our collective human experience. A solemn funeral alone is not enough. But a celebration of life that only focuses on the positive does not always go deep enough either. Allowing grief and gratitude to live side by side honoring both the love and the pain is a more accurate and authentic way to walk through the challenge of deep loss.

Death rituals are important for a number of reasons:

The ritual of a funeral or memorial service acknowledges the reality—and finality—of death. When a loved one dies, it can feel surreal, as though living in an alternate reality. Denial can set in, and one might think the person is away on a trip or asleep in the other room. Physically attending a funeral and seeing the casket or the urn with ashes can help shift from the feeling of living in a dream to the sad new reality of life without this beloved person inhabiting their earthly body. Burying my mother's ashes in the cemetery next to my father's had a very gut-wrenching and poignant finality for me. It was at that moment I knew I would never see either of them again.

It provides a safe space for deep grief to be summoned and expressed. People are expected to cry, to wail, and to express lament and sadness at a funeral. It is one of the few publicly sanctioned places in our culture where it is not only okay to fall apart but expected. The notions of "buck up" and "be strong" do not apply here. And thank goodness. A person may have to be strong to go back to work or help the kids return to school, but in the days immediately after a loss, it is healthy to express the full range of the emotional experience.

My friend Jon recounted a story of a funeral he attended where a young woman in her thirties was widowed and she cried and shook constantly, unable to walk unaided. In other circumstances, that might be viewed as excessive, but in the ritual container of her husband's funeral, it was perfectly appropriate.

It allows the immediate family and friends to receive support from their community. When a loved one dies, it can feel like the loneliest place in the world. But the celebration of life is an excellent place to allow others to tell what the beloved meant to them. People tend to come from various places in the person's past for funerals and share stories and happy memories of times with the deceased that can offer real comfort and healing for bereaved family members. It also brings people together from all different aspects of a person's life to share stories and recall fond memories of the deceased.

This is often when stories surface that some folks have never heard. It is a chance for laughter, remembrance, and joy in the contributions the person made to the world. I remember attending my father-in-law's funeral and how, the night before, we prepared poster boards with dozens of pictures of him at various stages of his life—as a child, a young man, a husband and father, a grandfather. I remember looking through his albums from college and noting that in almost every photo, he had a different girl on his arm. That led to several funny stories about his charm, the fact that he was a ladies' man, and how he was playful and a real prankster. I learned things about him that I had never known and realized just how much my husband was like his father—a man of strong moral character but always with a twinkle in his eye—and I was sad to think that he would never be around to know our children.

During the COVID-19 pandemic, many family members were denied proper funerals due to social distancing requirements and the inability of people to travel to be with loved ones. Often, the burials were private with just a few members of the immediate family in attendance. Like everything in 2020 and 2021, virtual platforms became both the default and the lifeline for connection and many people organized virtual gatherings to commemorate their loved ones.

The website www.whatsyourgrief.com is run by mental health professionals and offers great suggestions for people to host virtual gatherings including live streaming the service for people who cannot attend, creating a virtual slide show, singing together, and more.

Ceal, one of my friends and writing mastermind partners, hosted a virtual memorial service for her mom after her death during the pandemic. She lives in California, but her mother had lived in Mexico for more than thirty years. While Ceal helped to care for her in her final weeks, she never learned to feel comfortable around her mother. She recalled that hosting the virtual gathering was healing on many levels. Almost thirty people attended, and she invited everyone to say a few words about her mother. She explained, "It was nice to hear all the stories and to see people breaking into tears as they described their wonderful, intelligent, generous, protective friend who helped them in their careers or personal lives. It was odd to reconcile that idea with the angry, capricious, and sometimes cruel person I remember from childhood. But I'm glad I did it. It's nice to have closure, and to have provided some closure for myself, my siblings, her friends, and her partner."

The death of a loved one can be a challenging and confusing time, especially when relationships have been strained or difficult over the years. I certainly experienced that with my own mother as I have written about in this book. Designing a ritual can be a sacred way for grieving that helps to process the complexity of the emotions associated with a final goodbye.

Mourning Rituals after Death

Many traditions encourage people to wear black clothing for a period of time to let others know they are in mourning. For hundreds of years and in several countries, wearing a black armband has been a symbol of grieving the death of a loved one from queens, presidents, servants, military personnel, athletes, and law enforcement officers.[28]

In the Jewish tradition, sitting shiva at home for seven days allows time for the family to deeply mourn, away from the expectations of everyday life. Mirrors are covered, friends bring food, and the family receives visitors and talks about the loved one who has died. The mourners are fully able to focus their emotions on feeling and expressing grief.[29]

The ancient Greeks and Romans placed flowers on the graves of soldiers who died in battle as a way of honoring them. The belief was that if the flowers continued to bloom, the deceased had found happiness in the afterlife. We continue that tradition today by placing flowers and plants on headstones in graveyards as a way of connecting with our loved ones and taking time to pause and remember them.[30]

Public servants like firefighters, police officers, and military personnel are often honored by several traditions. At firehouses and police stations, flags are lowered to half-mast, black mourning bunting is placed around the building, and badges are shrouded with black tape or cloth. For a military funeral, there is often an honor guard, a 21-gun salute, and the presentation of the country's flag to a family member.[31]

Christian funeral rituals often include a service with prayers, hymns, a sermon, and sometimes music or poems. When a Muslim person dies, their body is prepared by being washed three times and then shrouded in three white sheets. The funeral is usually a very quiet occasion with no sermon or music and just quiet or silent prayers.[32] Hindu funerals usually involve chanting mantras led by a Hindu priest or pujari. But at the cremation, it is usually the eldest son who leads the family through the death rituals. White is commonly worn to Muslim and Hindu funerals versus black which is traditionally worn at Christian funerals.[33]

Grieving doesn't always have to be a completely solemn occasion. Irish wakes are considered one last party to honor the person who has died. After the body has been prepared and people have come by to pay proper respects, the mood can change as loved ones bring food and alcohol. There is often storytelling and sometimes even dancing and singing.[34]

In a tradition unique to the city of New Orleans, Louisiana, jazz funerals are a common way to celebrate and honor a loved one, especially musicians in the African American community. The jazz band accompanies the body by leading the procession from the church or home where the funeral was held, to the cemetery. Somber music usually accompanies the procession and more upbeat melodies are played after the burial is complete.[35]

Rituals to Help Prepare for Death

While my mom's final months were very private, by her choice, there are others who choose to host a "living funeral" which can have a similar feel to a milestone birthday party. Also called a "pre-funeral," it is usually hosted by someone who knows that death is coming soon, and they offer a chance for the one who is approaching death to spend time with beloved friends and family to say their goodbyes. The custom seems to have started in Japan in the 1990s as a way for the aging population to experience closure before dying and to provide support for their family members.[36] This concept has gained in popularity over the years as people realize what a shame it is to miss out on all of the nice things said at a funeral about the dying—why not be there in person to receive their praise and adoration?[36]

This idea of a living funeral was also popularized by the movie *Tuesdays with Morrie,* based on the book written by Mitch Albom, when the main character Morrie Schwartz, who is dying, decides to invite his friends and family to come to his home and make speeches to him that they would have normally reserved for his funeral.

Betsy Davis was forty-one when she died of ALS. She was one of the first Californians to use the state's physician-assisted suicide law and chose to end her own life in 2016. Before doing so, she hosted a two day Right to Die party where she invited friends and family to come celebrate her life with her. About thirty friends came and there was music, cocktails, pizza, and lots of laughter. Davis could no longer stand, and her speech was slurred at the end so taking time to plan her death was empowering for her after gradually losing most of her faculties in the previous years.[37]

When my mother's cancer returned just a few months before her death, I notified her friends and relatives. She had moved to Texas to be near us so I could help care for her, but most of her dear friends were in Florida. Over the next three months, she received the most beautiful cards, phone calls, and presents from those who loved her. No doubt if she had still been living in Florida, she would have had a steady stream of visitors coming to say goodbye.

Chapter Twelve: Death and Loss

She did a good job of preparing for her death. She organized her important papers and made notes for me about where items were located which made it easier for me after she made her transition.

We did not know it at the time, but she was sort of following the notion of the Swedish Death Cleaning method, which is a concept that has taken hold in recent years. It is the idea that once older (say over fifty), it is a good idea to declutter and simplify life so that upon death, relatives and friends will not have to sort through all the stuff. It is truly an organizational concept versus a ritual right before death; however, following these principles can certainly make life easier for loved ones left behind.

The Ritual before the Ritual

A few months before my mom died, I knew that I needed help preparing for her death. I got in touch with Marna, a spiritual counselor who had trained for years with shamans in the mountains of Peru. Marna is a powerful healer, and she suggested that I could help support Mom in her dying process by completing a series of rituals with white roses. She explained that she would energetically connect to my mom via the white roses and help to support her soul as it began the journey toward her transition from her earthly body to her spirit body. This connection would help my mom (and me, by proxy) to process her emotions about what lay ahead and would help her to release her attachment to her physical body.

Why white roses? Well, white roses are symbolic of eternal love and are sometimes called "flowers of light." We come from the light, and we return to the light. They also symbolize that love is stronger than death and also represent unchanging loyalty.

When I first arrived at my mom's apartment with a dozen white roses, she was delighted! But then I had to explain to her why I brought them, and what I wanted to do for her—with her permission, of course. I told her that I would leave them on the dining room table in her apartment for three days so she could fully enjoy their beauty, and then I would retrieve them and release them in the babbling creek by my home and say prayers and blessings over them in her honor.

Mom grew quiet for a minute and then said "Well, I can use all the prayers and blessings that I can get right about now… so, okay."

Over the course of six weeks, I delivered and retrieved three separate bunches of a dozen white roses and released each bouquet while standing on the wooden footbridge at the creek by my house. Every time I performed the release ceremony, I helped my mom work through her emotions, and I received support from the angelic realms to process my own.

With the first batch of flowers that I released, I experienced deep, gut-wrenching sobs of grief and anguish as I watched the stems sail through the air and land in the water. They remained bunched together as if holding onto each other for dear life. I suppose we were both in the stage of denial where we didn't really want to believe that she was dying. I prayed for Mom to have courage in the days that lay ahead, and I prayed for me to have the strength to support her and witness her in those final months.

The release of the second batch of flowers was a much more peaceful experience. It was horribly sad but serene and beautiful, too, and I felt very calm inside. Those flowers landed on the water mostly bunched together, but with two to three roses that separated from the rest. At this point, reality had set in that this was the course Mom was traversing. I believe we were both depressed and resigned to her fate.

When I released the third set of flowers, it was a joy-filled experience. I was smiling and happy and felt so much joy and love as I prayed over those flowers. During that release, the roses scattered like Pick-Up Sticks. I suspect Mom was ready to be free from the pain and suffering she was experiencing, and I started to see her imminent death as a celebration of sorts—she had come here to do her work and learn her life lessons, and it was time to graduate and return home. By that point, she had come to a state of acceptance with her death, and so had I.

The day after Mom died, a dear friend suggested that I host a gathering at my home, and I intuitively knew it needed to involve white roses. I quickly put together an online invitation and sent it to my friends, making sure that they understood that our time together was not just going to be about my mom, but about all of our mothers. I called it the white rose release ceremony—which I wrote about in the introduction to this book.

Hosting this gathering just five days after her death was really a wise thing for me to do. When a loved one first dies, there is a tendency to be in shock and not really process or function very well. But for me, an extrovert, I get buoyed and energized by being around people. Receiving the hugs and feeling the love from my women friends as they helped me honor my mother, truly helped me return to my body. It made her death that much more *real* and helped to steel me for the weeks ahead as we prepared for her more traditional funeral in Florida where I buried her next to my father.

Gravesite Rituals

When we attend a funeral and there is a graveside service, people will sometimes bring something to leave as a token of remembrance. Leaving flowers is popular in Christian traditions and placing stones is common in the Jewish tradition. Military burials often involve coins being left on a headstone as a sign of respect, letting the family of the deceased know that someone stopped by to pay their respects.[38]

Placing items in a casket is another beautiful way to communicate love and respect to the deceased. Throughout history we have seen this in tombs around the world, perhaps the most famous being the elaborate tombs in Egypt. King Tutankhamun's tomb was famously opulent with gold, jewelry, clothing, weapons, statues, and even a chariot.[39]

In our Western culture, the tradition continues for everyday people, but the offerings are usually a bit more modest. People leave everything from photographs to stuffed animals to books to cherished sports memorabilia.

Many years ago, our larger-than-life neighbor Mr. Cliff, who absolutely adored itty bitty Riley (he raised boys, but he and Riley had a very special bond), passed away and his wife and sons buried him with his favorite Rush T-shirt and a "love rock" that our daughter Riley had given him when he was sick, to let him know we'd been thinking of him and praying for him.

My colleague Kay had fifteen of her cousins attend the burial of her mother/their grandmother. Each person was invited to bring one small token that they thought represented their relationship with their mother. They shared the significance of each item and then they were all placed in her casket.

And when my husband's beloved dad Earl died, through buckets of tears, Eric placed his own hard-earned Eagle Scout pin on his dad's suit lapel the night of the viewing to be buried with him.

Honoring the Death of a Pet

For many of us, four-legged companions are members of our family. Dogs and cats (and other creatures, too) give us love, laughter, companionship, and perspective. They make us laugh with their silly antics, and they comfort us when we are stressed and anxious. Although they don't use words, we find other ways to communicate with them, and the bonds of love and loyalty run strong and deep. When a beloved pet dies, the pain can be just as searing as when a beloved human dies. It is important to create sacred space to honor their life whether it is during their final days or after they have actually passed.

When our sweet golden retriever mix Andy was dying years ago, my husband was a basket case. He and Andy had found their way to each other after my husband's divorce from his first wife

Chapter Twelve: Death and Loss

and they were bonded at the hip—a bachelor and his dog. They went for long walks, often just the two of them, and Eric would spend hours throwing the ball for Andy; he'd run circles around our backyard. In fact, in the early days of our marriage we would sit down to watch television in the evening and Eric and Andy would snuggle up on the couch together while I was relegated to an armchair across the room. After a few months, I realized I needed to change the dynamic and inserted myself on the couch between them, and finally Andy found his place nestled between our feet each evening.

When Andy was dying, Eric was beside himself with grief. The day before we took him to be euthanized, we both took the day off from work. We spent hours with Andy feeding him bits of chicken, lying on the grass in the sun, and telling story after story about his romps and adventures over the previous fifteen years. He loved to play in the snow, and he'd go running through the tall grass in the fields at our farm with only his plumed tail in sight. When he was older and he had lost most of his hearing, he would lie in the sun at Riley's feet, then a toddler, and she would "read" stories to him in her baby talk.

Author and journalist Jon Katz wrote in his book *Going Home: Finding Peace When Pets Die* about an Iraq War veteran named Harry who gave his beloved dog Duke one more Perfect Day when he knew the end of his life was near. Harry spent the day pampering Duke, a border collie/shepherd mix, with all of his favorite things: hamburgers and bacon, chasing his favorite red balls, going for a slow ambling hike, swimming in a local pond, and snuggling on the couch while Harry watched a movie in the evening. When Duke died a few weeks later, Harry felt comforted by the fact that they had spent one final Perfect Day together.[40]

Social media allows us to share our grief in a public way. Pet lovers unite and offer support and encouragement when someone's furry friend is faced with illness or passes away. It gives us the opportunity to share photos and stories about the life of our beloved pet which creates space and a platform to process the grief and loss, especially since we don't often have pet funerals, or if we do, they are very private.

We lost five pets over an eight year period—dogs Andy and Daisy, and kitties Percy, Graham, and Jasper—and with each passing, I took time to memorialize them all with loving recollections and stories. It is especially fun to hear from friends who knew them and their sweet spirits. It is amazing the ripple effect that the love for our animals can have on the people around us. I have certainly cried over the death of my friends' pets either because they had touched me in some way, or I knew how profoundly they had enriched the lives of my friends.

When executive coach Nancy Marmalejo lost her beloved Orange Kitty, she wrote a beautiful tribute to his life and legacy on Facebook. Orange Kitty was well known in his neighborhood and people would stop by Nancy's porch just to visit with him. He was a bit of an internet sensation as Nancy's clients and colleagues around the world followed Orange Kitty's antics for years. As a fellow ginger cat lover, I had known and loved Orange Kitty virtually for years. Here's what she wrote about him:

It's with a heavy heart that I share the news that Orange Kitty transitioned on Saturday Oct 9. He took himself to a favorite spot in the medicine garden, between the white sage, rue, and rosemary to welcome the passage.

He lived a good, long life (we think he was either nineteen or twenty). He served as my daughter's sibling, our front porch guard, provider of decapitated critters, man of the house, and protector of the realm from his perch on the front steps.

He introduced us to our neighbors by inviting himself into people's houses, commanding an audience in our front yard, and going up to any passersby with a request to be petted. Everyone complied and fell in love with him.

Many of you on Facebook have enjoyed my stories over the years of his love, cuddliness, companionship, and discreet gangsta style. He converted many cat-haters into cat-lovers, seeing everyone as a source of petting, ear scratching, and love.

He was an abandoned cat who found us and made us his forever family. He serves as a reminder that the Divine shows up in our lives in many forms, never to assume someone is less than because of their appearance or perceived importance in the world. He touched many hearts and I miss him.

We're quietly grieving, remembering, lighting candles, and sending blessings to him on his new journey as an Ancestor.

Rest in Power Orange Kitty

Planning a Grief Ritual for People or Pets

Here are a few things to consider when planning a grief ritual for a major loss:

- **Who is going to help you plan a ritual gathering?** It is extremely important in the days leading up to and after a major loss to garner support from loved ones who can rally around and provide emotional comfort as well as practical, tangible, hands-on assistance. If you are a member of a spiritual community, remember to call on your minister, rabbi, or other spiritual counselor for guidance. If a friend or relative is particularly gifted in offering empathy and creative ideas, engage their help to brainstorm ritual ideas.

- **Consider what kind of a ritual you want to create.** Is it something you are creating for the immediate family, or does it include members of the community as well? Did your loved one leave behind any specific wishes? If saying goodbye to a cherished family pet, what do the children need to experience to feel closure as well as the adults? If you are planning a traditional funeral or celebration of life, you may get support from your spiritual community and the funeral home for how to prepare arrangements. If you want to design something more personal and organic, you may have more flexibility to be out of the box.
- There are plenty of elements that you can include in your ritual:
  - **Photographs**—You can make a memory board of different stages of the person's life. It is healing for family members to create them, and it is special for attendees of the ritual to remember their loved one in happy times.
  - **Personal stories and anecdotes**—Whether writing a personal eulogy or opening a circle for people to share stories that they recall about the loved one who has died, recounting important milestones and sweet memories is a healing part of any gathering.
  - **Sensory elements**—Including the deceased's favorite flowers, foods, and music is a fun way to remember them and feel their spirit present at the gathering. When my friend Amy's husband, Kevin, died, they played "Sweet Home Alabama" at his funeral because he was a big Alabama football fan! More traditionally, "Amazing Grace" is often played at funerals, and there is solace in the familiarity of this hymn and the idea of peace after death.

- **Spiritual or inspirational readings**—When we are processing deep grief and sadness, we are often soothed by familiar words with messages of hope. Psalm 23 is a popular funeral reading as many find comfort in the promise of God's support during dark times as we face the challenges of life. Robert Frost's "The Road Not Taken" is a beautiful tribute to a life well lived.

Grief is a keen emotional response to a great loss. Investing time and energy in planning a grief ritual—whether it is small and simple or large and elaborate—is an important part of the healing journey. Processing death takes time and each step on the journey allows us to integrate the new reality of life after loss.

Chapter Thirteen
Women's Transitions

The female reproductive cycle is an amazing miracle of nature. Women populate the world and ensure the survival of the human species by their natural abilities to grow and give birth to babies. Starting a period as a young girl and aging gracefully into menopause are two universal experiences of women's life cycle changes that are worthy of ritual and celebration.

Sadly, so many of the rich traditions honoring women's life passages in cultures around the world have been lost in our more westernized upbringing. With the rise of patriarchy, women's changes have not only *not* been celebrated, but have even been made out to be taboo or seen as bad. As a result, many women have complicated relationships with their bodies and with their own sexuality because they receive mixed messages at an early age about their bodies. However, in recent years, we are seeing the reemergence of goddess energy and the sharing of feminine wisdom. Women are reclaiming their voices and their power.

Celebrating First Menses

Many cultures around the world celebrate a girl beginning her menses. In many Native American tribes, it is believed that women are more spiritually powerful during menstruation than at any other time. The Navajo tribe celebrates a puberty ritual called the *kinaalda*. It is a four-day celebration for the whole tribe because they believe a young woman beginning menses is bringing new life to the tribe. In Ghana, West Africa, girls sit under ceremonial umbrellas when they begin menstruation. They are brought gifts by family members and celebrated like royalty.

In several traditions, special foods are prepared in celebration of a girl's first menses. In Japan, a traditional dish called *sekihan* comprised of sticky rice and red beans is prepared for the whole family. In Iceland, there is a tradition of mothers baking a red and white cake for their daughters. In Israel, a girl is encouraged to lick a spoonful of honey to symbolically ease the pain of future periods, and in Croatia, a first-time menstruating girl gets to celebrate by enjoying her first glass of red wine![41]

Most young girls will start their menses between the ages of eleven and fourteen. It is a rite of passage for all females as they transform from girls to young women capable of creating life. Depending on the girl and the family, it is important to honor this milestone, but it can sometimes feel awkward or embarrassing.

Here in the West, many of us were raised with parents who used silly nicknames for our body parts and talked in hushed tones about menstruation. Fortunately, times have changed, and we now know that when parents speak honestly and openly about this natural life change, it can put everyone in the family at ease that this is just a normal part of life. Knowledge is power and giving your daughter the right information and attitude about her body can set her up for a positive, healthy relationship with her menses.

A ritual to celebrate this change in status can help the girl embrace this transition with grace and ease. It could be something quiet and low-key like a mom-daughter day (including sisters or aunties too if appropriate) to have lunch and open conversation about what it means to begin menstruating. It could be a gathering around a campfire with the girl, her friends, and their moms to talk about what it means to journey into womanhood. Or it could be a more lavish affair complete with a party and a playful-yet-practical approach to introducing girls to womanhood.

When I was growing up in Connecticut in the '80s, every summer my family would rent a little cottage for one week on an inlet in East Orleans, a tiny village on Cape Cod. It was a cute little bungalow that allowed us to look out at the water every morning and spend every day at the beach. I remember slathering on the sunscreen but still getting burned to a crisp with my fair, fair skin after spending almost eight hours each day by the ocean. We had many happy times in that cottage on the Cape.

I particularly remember the summer when I was twelve and a half because I got sunburned so badly that I couldn't even stand to put pajamas on. For the first time in my life, I slept in the buff. I was raised in a modest household, so that was an awkward and uncomfortable experience for me. I felt exposed and vulnerable, and on top of it, I was miserable because the aloe that my mom had slathered on me and the Tylenol that I had taken for the pain didn't quite cut it. I had a sleepless night.

As fate would have it, that was also the first time that I got my period.

I remember waking the next morning very distressed that there were stains on my crisp white sheets, and when I called my mom to ask for help, she arrived with a look of puzzlement on her face which quickly turned to pride and elation. She was thrilled that I had "become a woman," and as I stood there naked, covering myself partly with the sheet, I was mortified.

My mom had the requisite birds and bees talk with me, and of course, I had attended a health education class or two in sixth grade where all the kids learn about the difference between girls' and boys' bodies as they go through puberty. But other than that, we really hadn't talked about the change that I was about to experience, so it came as a bit of a shock.

Mom got me the supplies I needed, and I figured that was that. I got dressed gingerly and headed downstairs to breakfast. As the three of us sat at the table, my mom was grinning from ear to ear (something that I honestly don't remember a lot of from my childhood, so this particular time stands out in my memory as unique) and said, "Honey, I have an announcement to make."

My poor father's expression said, "What the heck is going on?" And I realized what she was going to say, but by then it was too late.

"Our daughter has become… a WOMAN today!" And she was absolutely beaming.

My poor dad took about thirty seconds to catch on to her meaning and looked appropriately shocked, bewildered, and clueless as to what to say before he finally mustered the words, "Um, wow, congratulations kiddo," and went back to eating his scrambled eggs. I wished desperately that I could sink underneath the table and disappear into the woodwork.

While I was completely embarrassed at the way my mother handled the announcement about my "womanhood," in retrospect, I'm also grateful that she made it a big deal in her own way. So many young women get the message that getting your period is dirty, bad, or wrong. Getting your period is a definite rite of passage for all young girls.

When it is my daughter's time to go through that life change, I hope that I will create a ritual similar to ones I learned from one of my lifelong friends and a former neighbor.

Whitney, my best friend from high school, facilitated a meaningful ritual celebration for her young daughter when she started her menses at age thirteen. They live in the beautiful Blue Ridge Mountains of western North Carolina where people are very in tune with nature, the cycles of the seasons, and the cycles of life. She invited her women friends and her daughter's peer group of friends. Some of them had already started their monthly cycles and others had not.

They began the backyard gathering by opening sacred space (they called in the four directions and any spiritual helpers) and they used smoke clearing to cleanse one another's energy fields. They built a roaring campfire and spent time singing around the fire before sitting in a circle.

The mothers began by sharing their own stories about how they were taught about their menses—or not taught, in many cases. They shared poignant stories about caring mothers, and they shared embarrassing stories about the first time that they bled through their pants. They talked about the importance of camaraderie that happens when one girl in school needs a pad or a tampon. As the mothers shared their stories, the other young women who had recently started their cycles chimed in with their more recent stories too. Throughout the evening, the girls were encouraged to ask questions and express concerns and worries, and everything was talked about in an open and loving manner.

After the conversation was complete, they all went skinny-dipping in the nearby pool. She recalls that the stars were twinkling and there was a feeling of love, validation, sisterhood, and being seen for this important rite of passage into young womanhood.

Whitney shared this with me: "I felt humbled. I felt shaky inside that my little girl was indeed growing up. I felt bliss with the other women in the circle and in awe that my girl was loved by so many and that she was *seen!* I was so grateful for every woman, and hearing their stories actually gave me new appreciation and new perspective on them, as women, and their life journey. I found myself wishing that my mother and her friends had done that for me. There was no talk of it or anything really… a few minutes of help outside the bathroom door trying to figure out how to use a tampon. That's it!"

At the end of the evening, each person attending was given a piece of jewelry. The mothers all received the same necklace and decided to wear it when they had their cycles so that when they saw each other in the grocery store they could have some extra compassion knowing that they were on their "moon time." The daughters received bracelets, and they were encouraged to wear them when they had their cycles as well.

Erika Busbee, a resident of Houston, Texas, got the idea for a period party after watching the *First Moon Party* video created by Hello Flo on YouTube. (If you haven't watched it, it is two minutes well spent! Link in Resources at the end of the book.)

She and her husband have two daughters, Aubree and Mandee, and they all thought the video was hilarious. They had many open conversations at home about this important change of life that all girls experience as they grow up. Then, Erika and her girls watched the powerful twenty-five-minute documentary *Period. End of Sentence* which is a short film about women in India fighting the stigma surrounding menstruation and ultimately manufacturing sanitary pads to help keep girls healthier and in school. (Link in Resources.)

So, when Aubree started her menses, the first of her friends to do so, Erika knew it was time to plan a party. Her goal was to make the event playful and fun but meaningful and educational too. She decided to throw the party in February near Valentine's Day, so it was easier to find red decorations. She searched the internet for recipes for red foods and they invited everyone to dress up in fancy red dresses. If guests wanted to bring a gift, they were encouraged to donate to the charity Days for Girls, a non-profit organization that supports proper menstrual health management. When each girl arrived, they received red hooded capes and were greeted warmly with "Welcome to the sisterhood!"

They played silly games, including Pin the Pad on the Uterus and a period-themed version of Pictionary. A neighborhood mom made a uterus-shaped piñata complete with fallopian tubes and ovaries and filled it with pads, tampons, panty liners, and candy-filled eggs.

A special "auntie" traveled from out of town to offer a tampon tutorial for the girls. She was both practical and hilarious, putting the girls at ease. She soaked the tampons in water to show the girls how they work, discussed different types and brands, and the importance of proper disposal. There was also a powerful discussion about respecting others when they have their period and the sisterhood that comes from knowing other girls are experiencing the same thing.

Even Aubree's dad participated in the party. He tended a fire outside on the patio, and at one point, all of the girls were invited to write down their fears and worries about starting their periods and then release those pieces of paper into the fire. One at a time, each girl had a chance to release her fears while the others chanted "womanhood, womanhood, womanhood!" in support.

One final gift that Aubree's parents gave to her was a crystal, moon-shaped necklace made from moonstone, a gemstone associated with new beginnings, supporting the reproductive cycle, and easing menstrual stress. Her mom wanted to remind her that she was in control of her emotions and wanted her to have a powerful talisman to remember her sacred moon party.

Another mom who attended, Barbara, said that it opened up an hour-long conversation with her eleven-year-old daughter after the party. They talked about how when a girl starts menses, she is capable of having a baby, but she is not ready emotionally to become a parent. They talked further about dating in the future, the importance of consensual touch, and how to set healthy boundaries. By having this frank discussion, Barbara hopes that her daughter will continue to talk with her openly about such personal matters and not simply turn to her friends during her teenage years.

This demonstrates exactly why community rituals are so vital to our health and well-being.

Erika may have planned this gathering for her daughter, but the ripple effect will positively impact *all* of her friends and their parents in the form of more open conversations, more honest communication, and hopefully, more respect for themselves and understanding of their bodies.

At the end of the party, Erika felt such love and pride for her daughter. She was thrilled that the other parents were so supportive, and it solidified the connection between the moms and daughters in their friend group even more. The other moms expressed their gratitude to Erika for handling such a personal topic with openness, grace, ease, and joy.

Erika observed, "It's my job to help my daughter feel safe and protected and feel comfortable having these conversations."

Ideas for planning a first moon gathering:

- **Consult with your daughter first.** Remember this is about her, not you. Ask her what she might like and what would make her feel uncomfortable.

- **Create a guest list.** Does she want a gathering of friends, or would she prefer some one-on-one time with mom and maybe some aunties or other mother figures in her life? It could be family only, friends only, or a combination of friends and family. Many parties include girls and their mothers together.

- Choose activities that feel appropriate for the occasion.
    - **Education**—You can read books, share videos, or if you gather a group, even have a guest speaker talk to the girls about health. Teach your daughter (and her friends) about proper hygiene and the choices they have

regarding pads, tampons, eco-friendly menstrual cups, period panties, and more.

- **Fun**—Laughter is the best medicine so playing games (they are still girls, after all!) will help the girls connect with each other and reduce their anxiety or worries about a potentially uncomfortable subject.

- **Connection**—You could invite mothers to share their first experiences of getting their periods, have friends write letters to your daughter, and encourage the girls in attendance to ask questions or share their thoughts on the subject.

- **Determine your budget.** You don't have to spend a lot of money for this ritual to be meaningful. Red ribbons tied in hair, red candies, or temporary heart tattoos could be fun gifts. You can choose to offer food to your guests, design it as a potluck, or hold it at a non-mealtime and don't include food at all!

- **Debrief the celebration afterward.** Soon after the gathering, be sure to check in with your daughter and see how she is doing. Ask how she's feeling, what she learned, and what questions she might have. Let her know that while the ritual celebration was a one-time event, you are always available to her for continued conversation.

Menopause

If we celebrate menstruation, it makes sense to honor menopause, too—the final major transition in a woman's body. When a woman ceases to menstruate, she shifts physically and energetically from her reproductive and mothering years to her wise woman years. It is often a time of reflection to think about what she wants to create and manifest in this new phase of life.

Many women who are post-menopause are thrilled to have no more concerns about possible pregnancy and having to manage their monthly cycles anymore. They savor the liberation. However, there are many women who go through the change and grieve the loss of fertility. As with many life transitions, there can be mixed emotions, and ritual is an excellent way to create a sacred container to experience all of those feelings.

Croning ceremonies are popular in pagan traditions where women celebrate the third and final stage of life, having transitioned from maiden to mother, and finally to crone.

In China, a woman's menopause is called the "second spring" which reflects their culture's feelings that this is a time in life for freedom. Many cultures revere their elders for the wisdom they have to share with the younger generations, and a croning ceremony can be a wonderful way to mark this threshold of change.

Elaine Mansfield, an author and expert on grief, created her own menopause ritual with a few close friends. On her blog, she shared that they went hiking into a gorge, and after arriving at the water, she shared these beautiful words as a sort of prayer. (Shared with permission from her blog entry "Gathering in the Gorge: A Menopause Ritual.")

"I offer my prayer to the fire and watch the paper transmute into flame and smoke. Then I continue the burning."

"Goodbye to the infants." (I throw baby pictures of my two sons into the fire, cringing as the flames tentatively lick the edges and then quickly devour the images of my children. Feeling remorse for the burned photos and the lost past, I plunge ahead.)

"Goodbye to the children." (I add photographs of my sons as young, preadolescent boys to the fire. The flame, knowing its part, consumes them quickly.)

"Goodbye to the mother-child couple." (I add photographs of my sons and me together, watching with cautious relief as the fire eats the images. I offer the next sentence with conviction and joy.)

"I welcome the young men who stand apart."

"Goodbye to the blood." (I throw tampons and sanitary pads into the flames, whooping and laughing without regret.)

"Goodbye to pregnancy and the fear of pregnancy." (I throw my diaphragm on the fire. A wave of doubt crosses my mind. *Is it ecologically correct to burn this piece of latex?* I let it go and enjoy watching the contraption melt and burn.)

"Goodbye to the woman who stands in relation to men." (I burn pictures of my husband and me before we were married and a picture of the family—my loving mate, our two sons, and me. A deep solemnity returns as I watch these images disappear. In silence, I pray for the protection and happiness of my children. I pray that, as my sons become adults, we will create supportive and loving relationships as equals. Finally, I pray that this transition will bring new opportunities for even deeper love and friendship within my marriage. I am ready to offer the final words.)

"I welcome the woman who stands in relation to other women."

"I welcome the Crone who stands alone."[42]

Ellen Dolgen is a menopause educator, author, and speaker, and she encourages women to have menopause parties. Her goals include reminding women they aren't alone, encouraging them to trust how they feel, and educating them to get the help they need. She believes strongly in having a safe space to discuss this important change of life that all women go through at some point.

She's started a movement called the Menopause Mondays Parties and offers it to corporate wellness programs so that women going through perimenopause and menopause have an opportunity to come together in a social environment and share their experiences with one another.

Do you feel inspired to create a menopause ritual for yourself, or help design one for a friend? Here are a few suggestions to get you started:

- Determine if you want the event to feel more sacred and spiritual or if you'd prefer to have a festive party atmosphere. That will vary from woman to woman and depend on your or her circle of friends and family, and who you/she may want to invite to the gathering.

- If you want your gathering to be more party-like, consider hosting wine and cheese, a girlfriends spa day, or host a themed Zoom party to connect with friends from all over. Google "menopause party ideas Pinterest" and "menopause party ideas Etsy" and you'll find all sorts of fun suggestions, including instructions for making a uterus cake, menopause party game ideas, and suggestions for making a hysterectomy survival kit. One especially fun piece of music to play is "Menopause Rhapsody - Bohemian Rhapsody Parody song for every Queen" which you can find on YouTube! Having fun and approaching this in a positive way is a big shift from the negative messages we get from society about what it means to get older.

- If you want your ritual to be more sacred and spiritual like a croning ceremony, choose a location that will support that energy such as a place in nature—a park, a lake, the beach, or on a mountain trail. You could also choose a retreat center, yoga studio, or meditation room that feels feminine and supportive. You may want to ask someone to facilitate the gathering, or you could invite participants to make contributions so it's a cocreated effort. Dancing, singing, and drumming are all encouraged. Take time to offer stories and reflection on where you've been—the joys and challenges of the maiden and mother stages of life—and then talk about the possibilities of this next stage of life as you step into your wise woman power.

Chapter Fourteen
Health

We all know the value of good health. When you are eating healthy, nutritious foods, sleeping well, maintaining loving relationships, and enjoying balanced mental health, life tends to flow along a bit more easily. If you are lucky enough to do enjoyable work and are able to balance it with play and rest, you can avoid burnout and approach your days with focus and clarity. There are daily health rituals that may help in maintaining vitality including regular exercise, stretching, deep breathing, eating whole foods, taking vitamins and supplements, and spiritual practices. You should also brush your teeth twice a day at least!

But life happens. Stress is a part of life and sometimes it gets the better of us. Unexpected events can occur that put our health, or the health of our loved ones, in a precarious position. Whether it is an accident, a surgical procedure, a chronic illness discovered, or a scary medical diagnosis, life can turn upside down on a dime.

At times like these, we may want to internalize things and push others away. We can be overwhelmed with emotions and unsure of how to express or channel them, so sometimes it is easier to keep other people at arm's length so you can soldier through on your own. However, it can be incredibly healing to experience discomfort and give yourself permission to extend your circle and actually let people in. Letting them see the pain, the grief, the fear, and the uncertainty can be transformative.

Professor, speaker, and author Brené Brown teaches that "Vulnerability is where courage meets fear."[43] Asking for help is a courageous thing to do. Whether it means asking for rides to medical appointments, allowing a friend to create a meal sign-up so that neighbors can bring food, or accepting the offer of a relative to watch your children for a few days so you can get some real rest. You can experience relief by simply knowing you are not alone, and the connection of the group is very powerful when facing major health events.

During the three-and-a-half years my mom was battling cancer, I engaged in the weekly ritual of writing on her CaringBridge site which is an online personal health journal. It helped me process the experience of what was happening, it kept her long-distance friends informed of how she was faring, and it allowed my mom a chance to receive messages of love and support from all over the country and then respond when she felt well enough to do so. It always gave her a burst of energy or put a smile on her face to hear from the friends she missed so dearly and maintaining those connections was an important part of her health journey.

At times like that, it can be helpful to engage in a ritual—or several—to help you or your loved one embrace the reality of what is going to happen next.

Designing a Health Ritual (For You or a Loved One)
- Consider your goals for organizing a ritual. Is it to offer prayers and support and set positive intentions at the beginning of a health journey? Is it to celebrate the

conclusion of a long ordeal? How do you want to feel at the end of it? Who do you want to include?

- Think about what would bring you comfort and care, inspiration, and hope. You could:
  - Facilitate a prayer circle in person or via Zoom.
  - Create an in-person gathering to receive physical and energetic touch to support your process and have friends offer Reiki or do a laying-on-of-the-hands ritual to feel empowered.
  - Do rituals with the assistance of Mother Nature (my personal favorite). Release roses in a nearby creek, burn paper outlining emotions you are ready to release in a ceremonial fire, play music and dance for joy, hope, and healing.
- Remember that rituals don't have to be large or elaborate to be meaningful and effective. Ideally, you want to create a gathering that helps you feel connected to yourself, to others, and to Spirit, and it offers a sacred space in the middle of busy days to process the reality of whatever situation you are facing.

Facing Cancer

Gail Kauranen Jones is a Cary, North Carolina-based author and coach who writes about her journey with breast cancer in her book *Cancer as a Love Story: Developing the Mindset for Living*. In it, she shares several rituals that she engaged in on a regular basis as part of her healing journey. She had surgery but opted to forgo radiation and chemotherapy in favor of more holistic treatments like dietary changes and mindfulness work. She attended weekly Tong Ren healing circles, participated in several sound healing baths, and engaged in a daily meditation practice as part of her healing rituals.

One particular ritual she found especially helpful was on the day of surgery for her lumpectomy. Friends from all over the country sent her an imaginary "pink blanket of love" at the time of her scheduled surgery. Gail says feeling that collective energy before the procedure, of the care and thought they were sending her way, felt so powerful and helped her know she would not be alone on that operating table.

The power of intention, particularly when held in a group of eight or more, is proven to be helpful, as noted in Lynne McTaggart's book, *The Power of Eight*. Gail's friends said they were so grateful she asked for their support as it helped empower them to feel they were contributing instead of feeling helpless.

Six months into her cancer healing journey, Gail participated in the renowned Mind Body Program for Cancer at Massachusetts General Hospital. It was there, in this evidence-based program, that Gail learned the significance of group support, in that those who participate in an intentional mind-body program versus a support group, can potentially extend their longevity beyond prognosis by two to two-and-a-half years. The power of community, where positive outcomes and elevated emotions are the focus, helps enormously. For that reason, Gail has led guided meditation groups to align people with the power of love and connection.

Another cancer survivor, Eileen Riehman, a physical therapist in Asheville, North Carolina (who also happens to be one of my best friends from our days in graduate school at the University of Delaware) discovered that she had uterine cancer and had to have an emergency hysterectomy. Just after that surgery, she asked some of our dearest friends to create a healing circle for her while she was recovering from the shock of the diagnosis and surgery and prepared to undergo grueling chemotherapy and radiation. This was at the height of the COVID-19 pandemic, so friends gathered outdoors in a park and stood around her six feet apart in a circle and shared their love, prayers, and blessings for her. She said it helped to bolster her spirits as she prepared for the next leg of her healing journey.

After that gathering, Eileen sent all the women in the circle a thank you gift in the form of a pink rose quartz bracelet as an expression of love and gratitude. Whenever I see one of those girlfriends, I always smile when I see them wearing Eileen's bracelet which is symbolic of our love for and connection with one another.

At the end of her cancer journey, after she completed her treatments, we hosted yet another ritual for her on a new moon once she was declared NED (no evidence of disease). Many of the same friends gathered.

During the ritual, Eileen first wrote down all of the fears, anxieties, worries, and grief that she wanted to leave behind. Then one by one, from small slips of paper, she read those concerns aloud and then burned them in a fire. Next, we hung a dragon piñata with the word "Fear" emblazoned across it, and we let her beat the crap out of it until she finally broke it and released the contents. Each one of the women had written their wishes and hopes for Eileen on this new chapter in her life. The positive words of affirmation and colorful metallic confetti rained down on her as she shouted with glee! She gathered up the words and put them in a jar with a quote that read "She remembered who she was, and the game changed."

Celebrating Moving into Optimal Health

Diana Kennedy is a Unity Minister in Unity Village, Missouri. She shared a unique health ritual—a smoking cessation celebration—for someone who wanted to celebrate the fact that she had quit smoking!

> *"A few years back, I had the privilege of leading a sacred celebration that was transformative, warm, and powerful all at the same time! As a minister I often lead programs and sacred services that warm my heart, but this one was*

special. This particular celebration emerged from a conversation I had with a woman I met in a healing circle (I will refer to her as Janine for privacy reasons). In the course of getting to know her, Janine, let me know she had just finished an eight-week recovery program for a yearslong habit she had wanted to overcome.

"*As Janine shared her journey with me, I could sense her joy, pride, and relief at having gone through such a powerful transformation while in a recovery treatment center. She was ready to celebrate the fact that she had quit smoking once and for all, and she asked me to lead a celebration ceremony for her success. Together, we created a sacred ritual where her support system could honor her journey of freedom from addiction.*

"*Janine welcomed friends and family into her home to be a part of the intimate sacred celebration held in her living room which included thoughtful, encouraging words, loads of color, cleansing water, and dissolving paper. After mingling for a while, I invited those in attendance to pause for a quiet, centering moment. After honoring the presence of the Divine, the ceremony commenced with each participant bringing to mind a blessing they wanted to share with Janine. The feeling in the room went from solemn to jubilant as Janine's loved ones each picked up a colorful marker and lovingly expressed beautiful intentions by writing and decorating special dissolving paper. One by one, friends and family members approached Janine, paused, looked her in the eye and spoke aloud a positive intention, and then dropped their paper wish for her into a bowl of water.*

"*As the paper dissolved, bright, beautiful colorful words floated on the surface of the water. The feeling in the room was palpable, the support, immense. Messages of freedom, peace, vitality, joy, release, and celebration created an enveloping energy of love and support for Janine that allowed her to step into a whole new beginning... As the paper continued to dissolve, she swirled the colorful remnants, which took on the look of confetti, reflecting back a feeling of celebration. Janine then took in a gentle breath and exhaled a sigh of relief. She had found her freedom!*

"The love shared with Janine that evening stayed with her and supported her on her journey for years to come."

Getting Ready for My Hysterectomy

When I made the life-changing decision to finally have a hysterectomy in January 2021, life had been extremely chaotic leading up to that point. We had moved from Texas to North Carolina in a whirlwind eight weeks (during the COVID pandemic), and then I solo-parented Riley for four months while Eric remained in Houston to wrap up some work commitments. As the gravity of the surgery started to settle in, I knew I needed some time away to be alone, to think, to process, and to prepare for this critical surgery. I booked myself a three-night getaway at the beach in a little studio apartment overlooking the Atlantic Ocean.

I officially kicked off my retreat with an opening ritual. I had brought some sacred objects with me and created a beautiful altar on the coffee table. I had several crystals, a candle, flowers, some energy-clearing spray, and my goddess cards. I opened the sacred space by beating my drum and calling in all of my beloved spirit helpers, ancestors, and guides to be with me throughout my retreat weekend. I prayed to them out loud for their wisdom, guidance, and strength to help me navigate whatever lay ahead. I pulled goddess cards to guide me through the weekend and was both surprised and delighted to invite the energy of the Butterfly Maiden (transformation), Kuan Yin (compassion), and Maeve (cycles and rhythms) to support me. Soon after, I spent time journaling with my uterus. I thanked her for serving me the best way she knew how and for the gifts she had given me over the years. I also journaled with my fibroids and endometriosis.

Here are snippets of my journal entries:

Dear Uterus,

> *Thank you for making me female, for giving me a chance to carry Life through Baby A and Baby B, even if only for a few weeks. Carrying those sparks of possibility and hope was miraculous and one of the highlights of my life on Earth. Thank you for regular cycles to cleanse me and to start fresh each month. Thank you for being the seat of creativity all these years and for being the Grand Pink Palace that carried those embryos for us. No matter how short, their lives mattered. I will miss you when you're gone but will do my best to keep the loving energetics of you with me and keep the creative life force flowing.*
>
> *xo, E.*

Dear Fibroids,

> *You, I'll be honest: I'm okay with seeing you go. You probably didn't mean to, but you've caused me a lot of pain and grief and wreaked havoc for as long as you've been around which is at least a decade, maybe more. Thanks to German New Medicine concepts, I understand that you grew as a result of resolving my conflict to not have a baby. You are the body's biological response via cellular growth. But I don't need you anymore. Uterus doesn't need you anymore. We're done. Settled up. You've served your role. Your pain and insistent pinging have caused me to be more*

in tune with my body which is good overall. I probably went to lots more acupuncture thanks to you which was good for my mind, heart, and spirit—not just my body! However, it's time to part ways. The toxicity and discomfort no longer serve me. There's a time and a place for everything. Now it's time to say goodbye. This is one life cycle ready to come to a conclusion. And on your way out, please take your buddy endometriosis with you. She's overstayed her welcome too!

xo, E.

Flower Rituals

In the healing work that I do with clients and for myself, we often use flowers to assist with healing, growing, blessing, and letting-go rituals. You may recall that I opened this book with a story about a white rose ceremony that I created to honor my mom after she had died. Flowers are a beautiful way to connect with Mother Nature and the spiritual realm in a way that feels nurturing and loving.

Intuitively, we know that different flowers evoke different feelings. Sunflowers spark joy and happiness between friends. Roses transmit love and compassion between lovers. Lilies can represent peace and serenity in times of grief. Of course, everyone has their own personal experience and association with flowers—some are more universally known, and others are more personal associations.

When I arrived at my beach retreat, I purchased three bunches of mini carnations in red, pink, and white. I think of red and white carnations as representing and loving both the masculine and feminine parts of us and I associate the pink carnations with feminine love and gratitude. This reminded me of the challenging days when I was in graduate school, working my assistantship and taking a full load of classes, and living on a very tight budget. I had to be mindful of excess spending in those days but one small way that I nurtured myself was to treat myself to one five-dollar bunch of carnations every two weeks. I always had flowers in my apartment, and this made me insanely happy. So, whenever I work with flowers (especially carnations) during rituals, it is a reminder of the importance of those small acts of self-love that keep us going during challenging times.

During my beach retreat, after I had written my letters, I knew it was time to do a release ceremony at the ocean. Under different weather conditions, I might have stayed at the ocean's edge for a long time, but it was freezing cold out. The wind was whipping, the sand was blowing, and I was pretty much isolated on the beach. Bundled up in my winter jacket, woolen hat, and mittens, I spoke out loud my prayers for the upcoming surgery, sharing my intentions to feel held, supported, and cared for during the entire experience. I thanked God, my angels, and my spirit guides for directing me to the proper health care team, and I expressed gratitude for my supportive family and friends who were preparing to accompany me on this journey. I threw the pretty pink blooms into the ocean and stood there for a few minutes to watch them drift out to sea then scurried back to the haven of my condo to warm up.

Creating a Prayer Bundle

When facing a health event like surgery, chemotherapy or radiation, renal dialysis, or anything else that requires regular visits to a doctor or hospital, carrying a prayer bundle can keep a person grounded and reminded that they are loved.

Having had surgery before, I knew that waiting to be wheeled back into the operating room is the hardest time mentally. It has the potential to be filled with anxiety and stress. I knew that I wanted to be calm, clear, and focused. My prayer bundle provided me with what I needed to achieve those states.

Here is what I placed in my prayer bundle bag:

- **Two rose quartz bracelets** given to me by two different women, which represented two different groups of friends. One was given to me on my fiftieth birthday at a sacred birthday ritual with my closest women friends from my days of living in Texas. The other was given to me by one of my lifelong best friends, Eileen, who had a hysterectomy just three months before I did.

- **A written prayer**. When I found out I was going to have a hysterectomy, I asked my girlfriends if they would be willing to hold space for me in a healing circle via Zoom, since I lived in a different city at the time. One of my friends was unable to attend, but she wrote the most beautiful prayer just for me. I read it to the women during the Zoom gathering, and we were all in tears receiving the powerful transmission of her love and intention. I printed out a copy of this prayer and tucked it into my blessing bag.

- **Baby socks**. Many years ago, I had a twin pregnancy that lasted just eight and a half precious weeks. One of my besties sent me a teeny tiny very soft pair of twin baby booties. It was the only baby gift that I was to receive since that pregnancy ended in miscarriage. I have felt those twin baby spirits as guardian angels over the past decade. As I headed into surgery, preparing to say goodbye to the womb that had nurtured them for a very short time, it felt important to have something representing them with me.

- **Crystals**. I also included a few of my favorite crystals: shungite for grounding, opalite for overall healing, and garnet (my birthstone) for courage and hope. I also tucked a seashell in that I collected from my recent ritual at the Atlantic Ocean.

I'm lucky to have so many beautiful women (and men!) in my circle of friends. Here is the moving prayer from my friend Ragan:

Sweet Jesus, great physician, word of God made flesh who was there at the Creation and brought the wonder that IS Elizabeth into being.

You know this woman.

Her heart.

Her mind.

Every cell of her body.

You know her fears and her pain. Make your loving presence known to her as she enters a new phase of womanhood.

Let her hear you rejoice over her journey with singing as she graciously and gracefully steps into what is next with deep gratitude for all her body has done for her so far.

Protect her.

Heal her.

Guide the team of doctors and nurses who care for her.

Bolster her sweet husband so she can lean hard and give precious Riley peace, calming any worries or fears she has for her mama.

Gently remind us all to cast our anxiety on you and accept your peace in its place. And guide us and give us all comfort, mercy, and grace as we navigate the great unfolding of our lives.

Lord, all change is hard. And "The Change" is no joke.

Send women along Elizabeth's path who can empathize and have enough perspective to know not all journeys are the same. And help Elizabeth use her experience, as she so often does, to be a blessing and guide to others.

I ask all these things as someone who loves Elizabeth and is certain you love her far more. Amen.

I hope this personal glimpse into my prayer bundle offers ideas for creating one for yourself, if you need it, or for suggesting this idea to a friend. You can choose anything that feels good to add to the prayer bundle:

- Something from nature like a rock, an acorn, a stone, a dried flower, or a feather.
- An item from a loved one perhaps children's artwork, a friendship bracelet, or a photograph.
- Jewelry or prayer beads like mala prayer beads, a St. Christopher medal (Catholic saint for protection), a meaningful piece of jewelry.
- Anything that helps a person feel connected to God/Spirit/Universe and the family and friends who love and support them.

Chapter Fifteen
Business and Career

By now, we understand the value of rituals in our personal lives, but can celebrating also make a positive impact in the workplace? Absolutely! Rituals and celebrations at work can enhance productivity and morale, inspire a sense of commitment to the bigger vision, and increase feelings of belonging in the community of colleagues. Let us explore some ways to bring more meaning and magic to the workplace, whether it's a large organization or a solo venture.

Large Organizations and Small Businesses

In corporate culture, a standard way of inspiring workers is to express appreciation to employees. This can include giving prizes for meeting sales goals, presenting recognition awards for years of service, and hosting lavish retirement parties at the end of a distinguished career.

One of my clients is BASF, the German chemical giant. They have a recognition program called "Recognize YOU" where employees can earn points (and ultimately prizes) when their coworkers or supervisors recognize them for doing a good job, going above and beyond, or for reaching service milestones. While individuals are the recipients of the rewards, the program builds community by encouraging workers to look out for one another and intentionally express their appreciation to their colleagues and teammates.

Howard Schultz, former CEO of Starbucks, wrote in his book *Pour Your Heart Into It* about the ceremonial taste testing they offer when onboarding new employees.[44] And Massachusetts-based moving company, Gentle Giants, hosts a ritual run up the steps at Harvard which corresponds with the company's values of hard work.[45]

Other organizations host annual bring-the-kids-to-work days, holiday parties, and pumpkin carving parties to introduce more play and fun into the workplace. Many Chinese companies begin the day with morning rituals for employees that can include movement or exercise, music, or listening to a pep talk. The intention is to help people transition from home to work and to help them feel connected to their fellow employees.[46]

In recent years, many organizations are focusing resources on developing their company culture, referring to the shared values, practices, and goals they want to infuse into the workplace.

Houstonian Leah Phillips, an employee at UnitedHealth Group, is a "culture ambassador" within her company. The company has a multi-day culture workshop every year and monthly calls with inspirational speakers for the culture ambassadors each month. The ambassadors use what they have learned to nurture employee attitudes and satisfaction at work. They start team meetings by inviting people to say what they are grateful for at that moment. It is a positive and uplifting way to kick off any meeting!

Small businesses have the freedom and opportunity to easily incorporate rituals into their regular activities. Roeder Orthodontics in Asheville, North Carolina has a great work environment that

Chapter Fifteen: Business and Career

team members attribute to their daily ritual. Dr. Roeder, a successful orthodontist in practice for twenty-plus years, is an enthusiastic believer in the principles of the book *FISH!* by Stephen C. Lundin, Harry Paul, and John Christensen, and he has each new employee read the book before starting work at his practice. Then he incorporates the *FISH!* principles in the office culture by establishing a "morning huddle."

During this time, employees gather to review the day's schedule and talk about any special situations or patient needs that require attention. After reviewing the day's business, staff members rotate leading the morning's inspirational activities. It can be anything uplifting like reading positive literature or something silly like handing out lottery tickets. The meeting ends with a short prayer and then a big cheer, "Let's go have a great day!"

Here are some simple ideas to incorporate community-based rituals that can make work more fun:

- Start staff meetings with expressions of gratitude (could be personal or professional) or recognizing colleagues by saying thanks.
- Celebrate birthdays, work anniversaries, or promotions with the company (especially if it's fun or silly or out of the ordinary).
- Hand out a coveted trophy or award when someone does a random act of kindness—and move it around the team every week or month so it is a ritual that people look forward to.
- Food rituals of bringing breakfast or lunch into the office when a team hits monthly goals is an easy way to build connection.

Solopreneurs

Personal daily rituals are known to be very popular for solopreneurs. It can be hard to stay motivated when working alone, so having a series of regular rituals helps a person to stay focused and inspired. Small actions taken consistently over a long period of time can help achieve positive results. One might think of them as good habits but the more meaningful ones meander into the ritual category. Popular rituals include a morning "power hour" to plan the day, doing yoga or exercise each morning, listening to an inspirational podcast during breakfast or on the way to work, savoring a perfect cup of coffee or tea, taking the family dog for a walk when the sun is rising, or saying prayers and setting intentions for a positive and productive day.

But garnering support from the community can be especially important when beginning a new and daring adventure. Susan Curington in Portland, Oregon, hosted a ritual surrounded by a circle of friends when she shifted gears from having her art be a hobby to becoming her full-time business.

"I know about the power of ritual, and I wanted to involve people that I trust and love to help usher in the change. I handpicked people that I knew could hold space for me, knowing that several of them were undergoing their own transitions as well. A friend originally offered to host a celebratory party for me at her lovely home, but as I leaned into it during the planning process, it became more of a 'launch ceremony.' Nine women attended, many of whom didn't know each other. After I welcomed everyone and offered an invocation, I paired people up and invited them to get to connect by answering two questions: What do you love? If you could do anything, what would it be? Then they had the chance to introduce each other to the rest of the group.

"Next, I read My Ideal Life vision aloud so that they could hold that vision for me with my new business as a full-time artist. Then I invited the women in the circle to share their dreams. Before the gathering, I had asked everyone to

prepare their own personal Life Wish List with twelve items on it. We took the first six and cut them up into strips of paper and passed them around in a bowl. We randomly drew from the bowl and read a Wish List item aloud. There was great energy and excitement in hearing one's dreams spoken by others. Then we took the second set of six wishes, and we each read our own slowly and deliberately.

"*When each woman got to the biggest, most important desire, she stood up and stated it out loud and then the circle reflected it back to her. So, I said, 'I am a full-time professional artist bringing upliftment and inspiration to the world through my art.'*

"*The circle responded by saying, 'Susan, we see you being a full-time professional artist bringing upliftment and inspiration to the world through your art.' After everyone finished their declarations, we held hands and prayed for these desires to come to fruition, and we closed our ceremony. We had a delightful potluck meal together afterward.*"

When I asked Susan about the tangible outcomes of the ritual for her, she said "I could feel the identity shift in my bones to *I AM AN ARTIST* almost immediately, and it took just a few weeks to really solidify." She also said that she appreciates the accountability aspect of the gathering because now when these friends see each other out and about, they ask "How's it going with your Wish List?" so the ritual has had a ripple effect of inspiring each woman in attendance to take even more action steps toward their dreams.

Susan still has two other businesses on the side that she runs with her husband, but her main gig now is her painting. "Art is blissful and joyous for me!"

Conversely, it can be valuable and healing to perform rituals when it is time to either sell a business or close it down. Many entrepreneurs have the experience of feeling like their business is a separate entity and has a soul of its own. Ending that long-term relationship properly is really important, just like one would with a real human person. It's important to acknowledge how a person grew, what was learned, celebrate the successes, and release what no longer serves each person.

When Whitney Natiello, an acupuncturist for almost twenty years in Swannanoa, North Carolina, was ready to sell her practice, she enlisted the help of a shamanic practitioner friend who invited her out on her boat, and they cocreated a ritual together on a beautiful sunny day at Lake James. Whitney thanked her practice for supporting her and her family. She talked to her friend about all she had learned as a business owner, a health care practitioner, and a wellness center owner. She spoke aloud her celebrations and released her regrets. Then, in harmony with Mother Nature, they performed a flower release ritual into the lake at sunset, the perfect time to symbolize letting go.

Whitney recalls "I remember feeling huge relief engulf me as dark descended and we drove the boat slowly back to the dock. Ritual provided me with the container of sacred time and space, out in nature with a trusted friend, to acknowledge all the roles I played for myself and others in my work life. That afternoon was a life-work review. I was able to acknowledge the good, the bad, and the neutral. I acknowledged the Divine perfect being yet imperfect human that I am. I celebrated the impact that I had and acknowledged there was more I wish I had done. By releasing all of that with reverence and respect, I opened the creative space to design the future I want to create in the next chapter of my life both personally and professionally."

Retirement is similarly a powerful time for ritual and celebration. We used to think of retirement as "retiring from the world" but now it is considered an exciting transition to embrace

Chapter Fifteen: Business and Career

the freedom, fun, and possibilities that come with this life change. We identify so strongly with what we *do* in our culture that it is important to reclaim our value as someone who is *be*-ing in the world.

Melissa Stanz hired me to facilitate a retirement ritual for her when she closed her business after two decades as a marketing consultant. I coached her through the process as she considered who she wanted to invite, where she wanted to host it, and what her goals were for this sacred space and time together.

Although her network is large, Melissa chose to invite a small group of women with whom she had worked intimately over the years. I emailed them thoughtful discussion questions ahead of time, so they knew the agenda for our time together and were prepared to speak about their trusted friend and colleague. We gathered on a chilly winter day at the barn where she kept her horse Booker, who of course was the star of the show when we first arrived! We reviewed and celebrated her accomplishments, we took turns sharing our personal experience of her gifts and talents, she declared her intentions for this new chapter of her life (pursuing training as an animal communicator), and we affirmed her vision for the future. At the end, Melissa gave each woman a custom Sacred Celebrations bracelet—made with onyx beads for strength, grounding, and self-confidence, and with a Circle of Life centerpiece bead as a reminder of our connectedness with one another.

Since establishing my coaching business in 2000, I have been a sole proprietor. Through the years, I have had collaborators and contractors working with me, but for the most part, I've been a solopreneur. It can be exhilarating being one's own boss, and it can be exhausting, too. Rituals can be an important part of keeping a business owner focused *and* help them to celebrate. When working alone, it feels great to achieve an important milestone (get a new client, have a banner sales day, etc.), but then it's a bummer to not have anyone to share it with at the moment.

One way for solo entrepreneurs to celebrate with others is to host what I call a "Gratitude Festival" on social media. I first did this when I was celebrating fifteen years in business. Daily for four weeks online, I shared personal stories about the mentors, coaches, and colleagues who have influenced my life and detailed the specific aha moments or takeaways that I gathered from my time with them. I thanked the amazing clients that I'd had the privilege of serving through one-on-one coaching, group coaching, networking groups, workshops, training, retreats, speaking engagements, and more.

Clearly my celebration style is *enthusiast*, so it was great fun to wake up each day knowing that there was someone new I was going to reach out to. The key to making it engaging is by telling stories with sensory details and photographs. Share the story of an inspiring client who made exponential changes, and what a privilege it was to partner with them on their journey. Or tell about another person who helps others consistently. Shine the light on others, tell their stories and your small role in their accomplishment, and thank them for allowing you to be part of it.

Of course, a minimalist could still do this ritual every year on the anniversary of their business by making a special gratitude post on the anniversary date and could simply add a byline to their email signature saying, "Celebrating ten years in business this year!"

However, I will add that there is a side benefit to this public display of affection with the compounding impact of social media. Public gratitude really showcases connections. People may not realize the organizations and people that a solo company comes into contact with locally, regionally, or nationally, so sharing stories from all aspects of business life helps them make connections and see the bigger picture of what the business does, its offerings, and how the product or service makes a difference in the world.

A great time to host a Gratitude Festival is anytime there is a big business milestone (five, ten, fifteen, twenty-plus years in business), or where there has been a recent big accomplishment—company expansion, book release, launch of a new product, office opening, or team expansion.

Here are some quick tips for an effective Gratitude Festival:

- **Choose a theme.** Each week (or each day of the week) can have a focus such as: mentors, colleagues, clients, personal connections.

- **Celebrate using social media.**
  - Tell funny, memorable, or impactful stories using Facebook, Twitter, Instagram, and LinkedIn.
  - Give someone a shout-out for their business on Facebook or Twitter or give them a glowing recommendation on LinkedIn.
  - Share photos from previous events or experiences and explain in sensory detail any memories about that special occasion.

- **Send something in the mail.** Handwritten notes or personalized cards are a great way to express a heartfelt thank you. Online systems like Send Out Cards, TouchNote, InkCards, and Snapfish even allow you to include photos or small gifts.

- **Pick up the phone and *call* someone.** We are so reliant on electronic technology these days that having an old-fashioned chat on the telephone is sure to brighten someone's day.

Part Three
Rituals for Daily Living

Major life events can occur years or even decades apart. We may have a series of major transitions in a short period of time or things may remain relatively stable on a plateau for years. But there are plenty of cycles that we face on a regular basis: waking up and going to sleep, beginning and ending a work or school day, and navigating the seasons and the holidays. Daily, weekly, and monthly rituals can help us stay grounded, centered, and focused on our values and on what matters most.

When we think about the quality of life we want to create or the legacy we want to leave for our children and grandchildren, creating daily, smart, self-care rituals are a key component. For many of us, our ancestors didn't have the luxury of carving out time for daily rituals. Many of them dealt with famine, poverty, abuse, oppression, bullying, The Depression, or war. For some of our parents and for many of our grandparents, life was very hard. It was a struggle every single day just to make enough money to keep a roof over their heads, put food on the table, and clothes on their backs for school, if they were lucky enough to be educated.

Life is different now, but many of us continue to model the behaviors from past generations. If children grow up with parents who are constantly burning the candle at both ends, caretaking for everyone else, never taking time for themselves, and ultimately getting sick because of it, those children learn that self-worth is linked to giving until it hurts and sacrificing oneself at all costs.

There is no doubt that we have more opportunities to invest in our emotional health and well-being if we choose. We then teach our children what it means to love ourselves, to respect ourselves, and to know our own worth. These children are going to inherit self-loving and self-reflecting behaviors that are positive, nurturing, and supportive.

Designing life with healthy, positive intentions sets up a great formula for success and rewards. There is a tendency to feel more energized, less stressed, more connected to loved ones and self, and with enough space in life to do the things that matter most. When actions that can be viewed as habits are viewed as ritual, those exact same routines take on a more sacred quality and they may become more protected as non-negotiables.

In this next section, we will talk more about some daily, weekly, monthly, and seasonal rituals that can easily be incorporated for positive results.

Chapter Sixteen
Morning Rituals

You've heard it repeated multiple times. The most successful people start their days off with a morning ritual. Morning rituals are good for our health—they decrease stress, boost energy levels, increase connectivity (to self, others, and Spirit—depending on the practice), and improve productivity.

Oprah Winfrey starts her day with twenty minutes of meditation and then at least fifteen minutes on the treadmill.

Tony Robbins starts his day with deep breathing, a gratitude practice, and prayer.

Steve Jobs looked in the mirror each morning and reminded himself of his dreams by asking himself, "If today was the last day of my life, would I want to do what I'm doing today?" [47]

Good habits are regular practices that we do every day to care for ourselves. One might say that traditional healthy morning habits include tasks like teeth brushing, drinking a glass of water upon waking, taking a shower, or making the bed, but adding some intention to these routines elevates them to a morning ritual. Plenty of people meditate, journal, pray, exercise, or drink a cup of coffee or tea in a mindful way that helps start the day off on a good note.

Creating a morning ritual will go a long way toward smart self-care. With commitment to such actions, one may face the day with more focus, a clearer head, and a calmer demeanor. Creating a morning routine for the family can help increase flow and harmony at home, especially for families with a lot of members.

Eric used to tease me that I require ninety minutes every morning to get going in the world. He was up, showered, dressed, fed, and out the door in forty-five minutes. Sure, I *could* do that, too. But I want to enjoy my day. I want to enter it consciously, not rushed or hurried, feeling peaceful, balanced, and focused. Having an established morning ritual allows me an easier transition from nighttime rest and awareness to daytime activity and rhythm.

My personal morning ritual has a lot of little steps but is actually simple. When I get up, I spend ten minutes doing yoga stretches on the floor. I usually don't turn the light on, and this allows me to transition slowly from sleep to awake. Then, I sit back on my bed, prop my pillow up, and meditate for ten minutes.

After that, I shower, and while I let the water cascade down my back, I do a visualization exercise to support my energy for the day. I imagine that my body is flooded with white light entering through the top of my head (my crown chakra) which fills my entire being. Then I choose a color for the day and pretend it is being poured like liquid gold into my body. Deep violet, turquoise blue, and emerald green are regular daily choices with an occasional pop of sunny yellow or tangerine orange. Next, I imagine that hundreds of little mirrors are wrapping up around my body facing outward, and I see the spaces for the good stuff to come in, but anything that's negative or harmful bounces off the mirrors.

As I'm finishing my morning ablutions, I mentally review the details of my day and get excited for what is ahead. After that, I dress and head into the kitchen.

At this point, I still have a half hour before I must wake my daughter. This is key for me because if my needs are met, I am in a better frame of mind to meet hers when she wakes up. I prepare breakfast, feed the animals, check email for anything urgent, then I go get her up. We have breakfast together, and we head out the door for the day.

Whew! It sounds like a lot, but it really is a flow that works for me. If I need a little extra sleep, I may skip the meditation. I rarely sacrifice yoga because it feels integral to waking up my body. I can always grab a shower later in the day. (Or wear lots of lavender oil! Ha!)

The morning ritual should be flexible. Weekdays, weekends, and vacation days will have a different rhythm. The goal of this is to have an intentional container for morning self-care but also know that what is in that container can be flexible and fluid depending on what is going on in life.

It is critical to note that your morning routine works for YOU. Not for your spouse or your kids or your mother or your best friend. What is it that *you* need to feel refreshed, renewed, and energized to take on the day?

Design Your Ideal Morning Ritual

You may want to grab your journal and take a few minutes to sketch out your ideal morning ritual or routine. Which elements do you want to incorporate? Consider creating an ideal morning ritual and an abbreviated one for when you have less time.

Getting a good night's sleep is critical to staying on track with your morning ritual. If you do not protect your sleep, then it is easy to hit the snooze alarm and then your whole morning routine is out of whack. How you do your morning is how you do your day, so the more consistently you can set yourself up for success, the greater the likelihood that you will stick to your morning ritual and reap the massive rewards it can provide.

First, think about how much time you have. Can you allot an hour or two just for yourself in the morning? Or does your ritual need to be short and sweet—perhaps just fifteen or thirty minutes? The stage of life you are in often dictates this. If you are single or retired, you may have more freedom in your schedule to choose what you would like to do.

Parents who are raising young children at home tend to have more demands on their time in the morning hours. They may feel like committing to a morning ritual is harder, but it is really even more necessary to start the day off right! During the COVID-19 pandemic, we also saw that people who stopped commuting and started working virtually gained a little bit of extra time for themselves each day. Dedicating some of that time to a morning ritual is a great way to set up for success.

Incorporate movement. Your body will appreciate having support in waking up after lying in bed for six to eight hours or longer. Begin your day with a simple stretching routine or some yoga poses designed to stretch and invigorate the body with a focus on meditative breathing. Tai chi exercises are also a popular low-impact way to energize your body first thing.

Invite stillness. Daily meditation is a wonderful way to transition from sleeping to waking. You can sit quietly in your bed, on a comfortable chair, or on a pillow on the floor for five to thirty minutes. Quieting your mind first thing allows for a calmer temperament throughout the day. If meditation isn't your thing, simply sit and savor your favorite mug of coffee or tea for a few minutes with no agenda.

Engage your senses. Stimulating your senses is good for the brain. When you play music, pet your furry friends, light a candle, or use essential oils, it stimulates different parts of the brain which in turn releases happy hormones to help wake the body up.

Welcome inspiration. Read something inspirational (a favorite book, scripture, specific intentions, or daily affirmations), step outside in nature for a few minutes and breathe it in, or talk to your angels, spirit guides, or dead grandmother, they always have good wisdom for you!

Design your mindset. Make a list of intentions, choose a theme, visualize each step of your day and how you would like it to go.

What NOT to do in Your Ideal Morning Ritual

Read or watch the news. Unfortunately, bad news dominates the headlines these days because the media companies know our brains are wired to be alert for danger in case we need to change our behavior. They capitalize on that knowledge and the news cycles are filled with gloom and doom. Don't allow that negativity into your experience first thing in the morning.

Scroll through social media. It is far too easy to get lost down the rabbit hole of your Instagram or Facebook feed. Instead, write in your calendar at what time during the day you will give yourself permission to enjoy some social media browsing—perhaps during your mid-morning coffee break or over your lunch hour. If you have strong willpower, maybe you won't hop on social media until your workday is over.

Did you know that in 2020, the average user spent two hours and twenty-four minutes per day on social media?[48] Imagine what you could do with an extra two and a half hours every day? You could spend more quality time with your family, fit in a workout, write more in your journal, and spend more time outdoors.

Go straight to work. It is critical to build in transition time in the morning. If you are at your computer within thirty minutes of waking up, you are not allowing your mind, body, and spirit time to feel fully restored after a good night's sleep, designed to repair, renew, and refresh your system. It is much healthier if you spend time with your family, do a workout routine, spend time outdoors in nature, or eat nourishing foods to begin your day.

Notable exception: My writing mastermind partners reminded me that for some creative types, heading straight to work upon waking is the only time they can find to write before the chaos of the day takes over. So, if this is you, go ahead and work right away for an hour or two, then reward yourself with a transition ritual into the rest of your day.

Chapter Seventeen
Everyday Gratitude Rituals

Gratitude, the feeling of thanks or appreciation, is an important topic in the field of positive psychology, an area of psychology dedicated to promoting well-being in opposition to the traditional disease model of psychology which focuses on how to relieve suffering.

Gratitude is about expressing thanks, feeling good, and acknowledging all that is well in the world. It is especially important to do this when life feels chaotic and stressful… a little bit of gratitude can go a long way in helping to find the way back to center. There are many well-researched benefits to gratitude, including increased happiness, better sleep, improved resilience, and better overall physical and emotional health.[49]

Gratitude rituals can be the simple things we do every day that give our lives meaning and invite us to take time to slow down and pause. Perhaps one might honor their ancestors by savoring the morning cup of tea in Grandmother's china teacup. Or maybe say the exact same prayer with the children before tucking them into bed each night. Lighting a candle on a spiritual altar and giving thanks for all the spiritual support they give is a great way to honor them. It doesn't have to be big to be meaningful and to help you cultivate an attitude of gratitude.

Both Eric and I are very mindful of teaching our daughter the importance of expressing gratitude. We believe it is important to live from a place of thankfulness and to count blessings every single day. In recent years, we have experienced several deaths in the family, and it has made us realize that every minute we have on this Earth is precious. Cultivating a regular practice of gratitude is good for the mind, body, and spirit.

Here are some activities that can help in staying focused on the amazing goodness in life, both personally and professionally:

- **Start a gratitude bowl or jar**. At work or at home (or both), start a practice of recording gratitude thoughts on slips of paper and then putting them in a special bowl dedicated to this purpose. It's a great tool to acknowledge loved ones for doing chores, and it is a place to express positive sentiments to colleagues in recognition.

  Once a week or once a month, have a team or family meeting to sit down and, one by one, review the expressions of gratitude and savor them again. It is a conscious way to connect with colleagues and loved ones and it is a terrific exercise to foster goodwill in the workplace and to teach children the value of sharing gratitude daily.

  You can also create a gratitude bowl just for yourself. You could put it on your altar or some other sacred place where only you will know what's in there. Thanking yourself for sleeping in, taking a wellness day, walking in the woods, calling an old friend, and writing in your journal are all sweet little whispers to keep the fountain of self-care flowing!

- **Express gratitude directly.** People like to be appreciated for a job well done, a goal achieved, a risk taken, or simply for being kind. Some easy ways to do this:
  - Give someone a shout-out on social media (Facebook and Twitter are great for this!) or a recommendation on LinkedIn, Amazon, or Yelp (depending on their business).
  - Send a heartfelt, handwritten card or a personalized gift that helps the recipient feel seen, heard, and appreciated.
  - Pick up the phone and call someone. (Not a text and not an email!) It is guaranteed to brighten their day.
- **Keep a gratitude journal.** This is a practice I recall having gained widespread popularity when Oprah talked about it publicly in the mid-1990s and has since become a fairly mainstream concept. Consider keeping one. It is an excellent discipline to help you shift the focus from what is missing in life to instead shine the spotlight on the abundance already around. Once I started keeping a gratitude journal, I became more open and receptive to the abundance of good flowing my way. Simply dedicate a journal to your gratitude practice and write down three to five gratitudes each day.
- **Replace traditional grace with *gratitude* grace.** I learned this one many years ago from my friends Shonnie and Bruce. I was accustomed to the traditional grace that is often said before a meal in some families, but when I was invited to their house for dinner, they encouraged me to chime in with my own gratitude. Each person goes around the dinner table and says one or more things that they are grateful for. It is a lovely practice to reflect on your day in a meaningful way and giving voice to the blessings sends a message to the Universe that people are grateful to receive, which tends to prime the pump for more abundance and goodness to flow!

Here are some prompts to get you started:

- What am I grateful for right now, at this moment?
- I'm grateful for this person I encountered today…
- I'm grateful for this experience I had today…
- Something I learned today that I'm grateful for…

Gratitude is a game changer.

As an ESFJ on the Myers-Briggs, my natural tendency is to see flaws and point them out vocally to anyone who will listen (the extrovert judger—we are good at locating the gaps and quick to say, "Look! There it is!"). I used to be a very critical person, often looking for the flaws, what was lacking, and the missing pieces of my life. My focus was on the negative, the difficult, and the obstacles. But once I plugged into the notion of gratitude and started noticing the positive, the easy, and the possibilities, things shifted. I started keeping a gratitude journal to record the evidence, and it helped me be more open and receptive to the abundance of good flowing my way.

As a result, I stopped being so critical, although I'll be honest, it is still a natural default, and it takes effort for me to correct. I correct myself a lot, often in my head, and if something comes out of my mouth and I don't like how it sounds, I'll pause and say, "Let me say that differently." I often improve my own language and invite those around me to choose different words as well. I can get away with that easier with my daughter and with my clients than I can with, say, my husband.

Seven Things to Remember about Gratitude:

1. It's always available to you.
2. It helps you be in the present moment.
3. It can shift a negative thought into a positive one, a difficult day into a better day.

Chapter Seventeen: Everyday Gratitude Rituals

4. It's an easy, cheap "happy pill" that doesn't require much time, money, or even exercise!

5. It helps you to feel connected when you are under the illusion that you are disconnected.

6. It plugs you back into Source energy.

7. It makes you feel good!

Dr. Wayne Dyer said, "Change the way you look at things and the things you look at change."[50] What he meant by this is when someone focuses attention on looking at the negative aspects of a situation, that is all they will get. But if they can see the difficult parts of the situation and also see the opportunities, they will start to see more positive options unfolding.

One of my coaching clients, Karen Dulyunan, a speech therapist in Sugar Land, Texas, told me during a coaching session that her daughters, ages six and three, were going through a normal kid phase of feeling entitled. She was feeling frustrated and taken for granted as a person and as a mom, and she asked me what she could do about it.

I suggested that she try a gratitude practice at dinner. When her family of four sits down to eat, they start off the meal with everyone sharing a special moment they want to express gratitude for from that day.

At first, she said that her daughters saw it as a competition. One would say, "Mommy read me a book today," and the other would say, "Well, Mommy read me TWO books today!" Initially, her husband wasn't on board either and would roll his eyes and share very surface-level expressions of thanks.

But Karen persevered. She continued to invite the family every night to share their gratitude and over time, she saw a real transformation occur. The girls got excited to come to the dinner table and share what they were grateful for, and they spent time choosing the perfect thing before it was time to eat. Even her husband started to settle into the practice as he saw the positive impact it was having on the girls, and soon he too was sharing meaningful words. And most of all, Karen felt acknowledged and recognized for her efforts in the family. She was relieved that she was able to help her family shift from an attitude of entitlement to an attitude of gratitude in a relatively short time frame with minimal effort.

Another client, Leigh Ann Mertens, a yoga studio owner in South Carolina, was experiencing apathy and disengagement with her teenage son. He was very introverted, and she wanted a strategy to draw him out in a way that felt safe and supportive to him. So, I suggested the idea of a gratitude bowl. She got a bowl and left it on the dining room table and put blank slips of paper and pens nearby, and during the week, as family members found something to be thankful for, they would write it down on a slip of paper and put it in the bowl. Then they chose Sunday nights as the night to sit as a family and review the gratitudes. In time, Sunday became the most anticipated family meal of the week as everyone experienced how nice it was to be recognized for the little things. "Thanks for taking out the trash." "Thanks for washing my car." "Thanks for making my favorite meal."

I remember how gratitude helped me survive the pain of my divorce two decades ago. I was miserable and heartbroken. But once I moved—I had to physically relocate, I believe, to experience this shift—I was able to see the possibilities for me and for my life. I was able to see that there was life beyond divorce. I took risks and made new friends (on a beach trip!), tried new activities (hiking, Nia), went back to church (Jubilee!), and even started dating again (that was weird at first! Then it got fun. Really fun!). I found my strength, my voice, and my truth again.

I had commented to a friend "I'm a new version of me!" and she said, "No, Elizabeth, you're really just rediscovering the real you—she's been buried these past few years." *Whoa.* She was right.

I cried every day for about three months. But each day, I found one small thing to be grateful for. Sometimes it was the smell of the leaves, or the view of the mountains, or the kind clerk at the grocery store or the sweat that I worked up at Nia class. And then, one day, I didn't cry. And then another. And then another.

I was able to see, in time (this was more like years, not months!), that getting divorced was an incredible gift in my life. An opportunity for growth, expansion, learning, healing, and more. I stepped more fully into who I was.

Chapter Eighteen
Family Rituals

One of the most important communities that any of us will ever participate in is being a member of our immediate family. The environment in which we are raised shapes our early experiences of love, trust, and communication and impacts our identity formation and who we become as adults. How often is it said, "My family does this…" when describing an event or tradition?

In addition to birthdays and holidays that are referenced in other chapters, let's look at some of the repetitive (annual, monthly, weekly, daily) rituals and traditions that can leave the most lasting impact on our loved ones.

Family Meetings

Open communication is often the goal for family meetings to get everyone on the same page about schedules or any issues facing the family. It can be a great opportunity for children to have their voices heard, and for parents to have focused, uninterrupted time listening to and engaging with the youngest family members.

Choose a special location to hold meetings (perhaps the back patio instead of the kitchen table) and create a ritual opening and closing activity. It could be as simple as ringing a bell, lighting a special "family candle," or pulling out a talking stick that gets passed around the circle as each family member shares what they want to say.

In addition to covering upcoming events and schedules for the week, include some sacred time. If the family keeps a gratitude jar, consider choosing to read the notes in it each week during the family meeting. Similarly, creating a prayer or blessing box provides each member a chance to write their thoughts and put them into the box. It can also be a great opportunity to say prayers and blessings or set positive intentions for the week ahead.

Dates for Adults

Whether or not there are children, it can be critical to the health and well-being of relationships to have regular date nights. Taking time away from the normal routine can help to improve communication, decrease stress, increase intimacy, and enhance connection. Going out is always fun—eating a special meal together, attending a play, watching a movie, or playing putt-putt golf can be fun ways to talk and laugh and get away from the day-to-day responsibilities.

But dates do not have to be costly to be enjoyable. Try taking a picnic to a local park to watch the sunset, eat ice cream cones while window shopping, or go for a hike out in nature. What is important is to get outside of the normal routine with no electronics, no responsibilities, and no distractions so the focus is on the two of you in the relationship.

My friends Danielle and Doug live in Halifax, Nova Scotia and are raising two young children. They do not live near family and securing a babysitter isn't always the easiest. They rely on "day dates" to keep their marriage fresh. They choose one day a month when their son is in school and their daughter is in daycare, and

Chapter Eighteen: Family Rituals

they both take the day off from work so they can go kayaking and have a picnic, enjoying adult conversation only!

Dates with Children

Adults aren't the only ones who can benefit from dates. When life gets chaotic and schedules seem to be running at odds with each other, children can really benefit from going on dates with just one parent. Especially for larger families where kids rarely get dedicated time with a parent, this can feel like a real treat and can instantly deepen connection. We only have one child, but even our daughter says that she really enjoys our mommy-daughter road trips, and she loves having one-on-one lunch dates with Daddy. Create an art project as a team, go see a movie and grab a milkshake afterward, explore a museum together, or go for a long bike ride. These parent-child dates don't need to be complicated to be impactful.

Game Nights/Movie Nights

When I was growing up in the '80s, game nights were a staple in many of my friends' homes, as were pizza nights and movie nights. We didn't have the distractions of technology (unless you count television and Atari games!) that are pervasive in our society today.

Too much reliance on our electronic devices is exactly why game nights are so critical these days. Choose one night a week to play family classics like Clue, Monopoly, Scrabble, and Pictionary or more modern games like Exploding Kittens, Apples to Apples, or Ticket to Ride. Playing games can help children sharpen math and language skills, learn the value of teamwork, and have healthy experiences winning and losing. Engaging with loved ones in this way creates shared memories, supports collaboration, fosters healthy competition, and generates lots of laughter!

Family rituals create a sense of belonging and a feeling of connectedness. They can also add to our identity. For example, some families have fun nicknames for one another. One such family lives in our neighborhood and the parents enjoyed watching the Netflix series *Money Heist* where each of the main characters had a code name based on a major city somewhere in the world. So, this family adopted the same concept, only each member has to use the initial of their first name and they can choose a city, state, or country. So, Amanda is Alaska, Erin is England, and Scott is Seattle.

Of course, there are plenty of other simple family rituals that can have a lasting impact on feelings of connection and consistency. Offering special morning and evening hugs and kisses, saying evening prayers together, planning an annual family camping trip, and volunteering in the community on special occasions are all good ways to strengthen the bonds of love among the people in the home. The key is finding out what works for everyone based on their personalities and ages, and then committing to doing these things on a regular basis.

Chapter Nineteen
Develop Your Own Prayer Rituals

A note about prayer:

In this chapter, I refer to God several times for simplicity's sake of how to refer to the Divine. In my personal practice, I often substitute the words Goddess, Universe, Creator, Mother Earth/Father Sky, or Higher Power. Others may prefer to pray to the Lord, Jesus Christ, Allah, Buddha, or other deities. I believe that prayer is about connecting with something larger than us, a Divine presence that we may sense or know. Please read this and substitute the words that most closely fit with your beliefs.

My parents didn't raise me with religion, and we never talked about God at my house. They made me go to Sunday school at the local Congregational Church for two years in elementary school and then asked if I wanted to continue going and I said no. I thought it was boring, so I stopped.

They never went to church with me, so my guess is that they thought I "should" attend, but their heart wasn't really in it. I do recall that we attended the candlelight services as a family on Christmas Eve, and I always loved the tradition of singing holiday carols, but other than that, my family was not spiritual or religious in any way.

My dad had a heart attack when I was fourteen years old, and it was the first time I remember praying. I knelt on my twin bed in the middle of my pink and green wallpapered 1980s room in Connecticut and started talking to God for the very first time. I remember feeling scared and worried as I rocked back and forth on the bed while I released my fears through my tears out loud to God, hoping I would be heard. The essence of my prayer was: "I'm not ready for Daddy to die. Please let him live, and I will commit to learning about you, understanding you, and having a relationship with you."

My dad survived his heart attack and went on to live for another ten years.

Soon after his recovery, I started asking my parents to let me go on a non-denominational retreat weekend hosted by a local church called Emmaus. A lot of my friends had attended and returned feeling happy, cared for, and loved.

My parents resisted for a long time. "Why do you need that? It's just a bunch of church-based mumbo jumbo." They were adamantly against it, likely because they didn't understand it or have any connections to it, nor did they understand MY desire for spiritual community, but they finally acquiesced and let me attend.

What I remember most about the weekend was the letters of love and affirmation that I received from family and friends. The organizers asked loved ones to send along a letter to participants affirming our gifts and why they loved us. We received the letters at different times throughout the weekend, and I remember feeling so loved and cherished.

Soon after, my high school boyfriend gave me the novel *Illusions: The Adventures of a Reluctant Messiah* by Richard Bach, and I was introduced to a completely different way to look at spirituality. This book introduced me to magic, miracles, and the idea of past lives. It piqued my curiosity to learn more about the nature of reality versus the illusions we may be living in. It was a critical catalyst in my spiritual awakening.

When I headed south to attend The College of William & Mary in Williamsburg, Virginia, most of my friends were shocked that I did not have a church that I belonged to. Almost all of them were raised with religion as a focal point of their family's foundation, so I was unusual. I had plenty of friends in high school who were religious—they were mostly Catholic or Jewish with a few Protestants. I knew an atheist or two, as well, but we never really talked about it.

The Christian pop singer Amy Grant was very popular at the time, and my roommate Debbie loved playing her music. I sang along with the tunes that were filled with joy and inspiration because they made me happy.

I became a seeker in college—I was curious and wanted to experiment, explore, and understand more about religion and spirituality. I asked my friends to take me to their churches. Over the years, I attended Catholic Mass and services at Presbyterian, Methodist, and Baptist churches. I had been to Jewish temple in high school because two of my best friends were Jewish.

One of my summer romances during college was a gentle soul named Derek who was Quaker. I still recall the silence and the peace that pervaded the meetinghouse, which may be one of my favorite experiences from that time in my life. I also remember my first job out of graduate school when I was working in Wilmington, North Carolina. I attended church with one of my student employees, a young Black woman named Ellen who went to the charismatic AME (African Methodist Episcopal) Church. I went with a few other Caucasian friends, and we were the only White people in the sanctuary. We were greeted with warm smiles and approving nods.

The church services that I had attended up until then were very solemn and quiet affairs, but the joyful singing and dancing of the congregation swaying in celebration of God's love was a new experience for me. It was such a joyful time and church actually felt fun!

As an adult, I pray daily. I pray alone in the shower each morning. I pray with my family every night when we say grace at the dinner table. I often pray when I'm out walking in the woods, and I'll talk out loud to God to express my thanks or to unburden my troubles.

Apparently, I'm not alone. Prayer is a daily ritual for much of the world's population. Pew Research Center data between 2008 and 2017 showed that 55 percent of Americans engage in daily prayer, but around the world, those statistics vary from 95 percent in Nigeria to 75 percent in India and 33 percent in Japan.[51]

We pray for a lot of different reasons. We pray to feel our connection with God and all that we perceive to be Divine. We pray for good health, safe travels, and clarity on our career path. We pray for good fortune, creative inspiration, and peace around the world.

Anne Lamott titled one of her books *Help, Thanks, Wow* in honor of the three most common prayers we say. We often seek guidance and problem solving; we regularly say quick prayers of gratitude and thanksgiving; and prayers of wonder often come spontaneously when we have witnessed a miraculous holy moment.

I remember reading Elizabeth Gilbert's *Eat, Pray, Love,* which came out a few years after my divorce. It was a time of serious contemplation and reflection for me, and she described praying as talking to God and meditation as listening to God. Ever since, that has made so much sense to me.

Making a regular habit of prayer can be good for one's health. Not only does it strengthen spiritual connection, but studies show it can also reduce feelings of anxiety and fear. It helps to calm the nervous system and helps to shift focus from the mundane to the metaphysical. I know when I find my brain getting caught up in the details of how to solve a complex problem, if I take a moment to take a deep breath and pray for clarity, I immediately feel better.

Think about your own prayer practice. What do you do now? What have you done in the past? How does prayer make you feel?

There are many ways to pray. Here are a few examples as you consider how you might like to incorporate prayer even more into your life:

- You can pray in a church, temple, or synagogue with fellow worshippers.
- You can pray in the presence of a priest, rabbi, spiritual counselor, or spirit mentor.
- You can pray while walking in the woods, soaking up nature, and feeling one with the All That Is.
- You can pray in the shower.
- Or at night before you go to bed.
- You can even pray on the bathroom floor after you have cried every last tear and feel spent, helpless, and alone.
- You can pray every time you get in the car to drive.
- Every morning when you send your kids off to school.
- Or every time before you stand up at a podium to give a speech.

Many were brought up expecting certain prayers, especially if their families were particularly religious. For example, prayer at weddings and funerals are commonplace, as are prayers at baptisms, over someone sick, and even at graduations. A family ritual for many has been prayer before a meal or at bedtime.

But think about how, even if a person isn't particularly religious, there is a certain reverence that can be felt in each of those situations. Consider the closing up of one home with a simple "Goodbye, we'll miss you" and the opening of a new one with

"Hello, we look forward to being good stewards of this beautiful space." Hold the moment with a deep breath and a heartfelt connection as you say your parting words or your invocation. By adding a little intention behind presence in most any situation, a prayer is established.

There is no secret recipe or standard formula that makes praying work. It's an ongoing communication with the Divine and doesn't have to be structured or complicated to be meaningful or effective.

Chapter Twenty
Home Altars

Altars have been used by religions around the world as sacred spaces for prayer and worship to present offerings, celebrate events, and connect with the Divine. Most of the world's major religions use altars in their churches, shrines, and temples. You may find religious texts, candles, flowers, incense, religious icons, water, bread, and more placed on an altar. Primitive religions likely used certain places in nature—a rock outcropping, a special tree stump, a fork in the river, a mound of earth—as natural places for gathering, sharing offerings or sacrifices, and connecting to the Divine.

Dr. Wayne Dyer said, "We are not human beings having a spiritual experience. We are spiritual beings having a human experience."[52] I agree wholeheartedly with Dyer. That's why building a personal altar as a spiritual touchstone in a home is a powerful act. This can be a place for prayer, meditation, and contemplation and a place to draw positive things into one's life.

We get caught up in the day-to-day of do, do, do and sometimes forget to be, be, be. Visiting an altar helps connect us to our spiritual center, however we define it. It's a place to land before, during, or after a busy day and feel safe, loved, grounded, and inspired.

An altar is a special place where we can place things that we love, items that bring us to tears, things that evoke special memories, and anchors of divine experiences. It can be on the nightstand, a bookshelf, in the meditation room (if you're lucky enough to have one), on the back porch, in the office, or in the garden.

I was first introduced to the concept of a personal home altar when I lived in Asheville twenty years ago. I remember walking into my friend Melissa's house, and she was giving me a tour of her space. She took me downstairs to her office, which had a beautiful view of the mountains from where she could do her writing and consulting work. She had a low square table with all sorts of interesting items on it.

I asked her what it was, and with a big smile, she said, "Oh, that's my altar!" She was delighted to share with me that there were photographs of loved ones who had passed on, several rocks and crystals, a few delicate seashells, and some feathers she had found on her hikes. There were chimes, a few goddess-type statues, and some artwork.

To anybody else, it may have looked like a mishmash of random things, but to her, it was a sacred place to settle. She told me that she would often just sit on the floor in front of her altar, pick up an item and hold it in her hand and pray or meditate.

Since that first introduction many years ago, I have been in several homes where there are altars.

- My friend Melinda keeps her altar in a beautiful hand-carved wooden cabinet, and it's only when she plans to meditate that she opens the doors and reveals the sacred contents inside.

Chapter Twenty: Home Alters

- My coaching client Susan has her altar on a low table right next to her bed filled with crystals, angel figurines, a cross, and artwork from her daughter. Hers also includes a deck of angel cards, and she pulls a new card daily to help her with grounding, focus, and inspiration.

- Another friend Kevin keeps a few sacred objects on the mantel of his fireplace, including some fossils and a brass figurine that belonged to his dad. It's not obvious that it is an altar, but knowing him, it is apparent that they are meaningful objects.

- My grandmother had an altar of sorts—a photo of her son (my dad's brother, Uncle Bill) who died when he was in his forties, and she always kept a fresh rose from her Florida garden in the crystal bud vase next to his image.

- My daughter Riley decided to build her altar on the bottom shelf of her bedside table when she was about six years old. She had seen my altars and wanted one of her own. She placed her love rocks, some seashells, crystals, and feathers she had gathered, and a photograph of us with her birth mom in the hospital, when she was only two days old.

Whenever I lead a women's retreat, I invite participants to bring something to contribute to the temporary altar that we cocreate together. When I facilitate the opening circle, I encourage each of the women to share their name, their intentions for retreat, and their altar item. People have contributed an array of items over the years—photographs of beloved family members, heirloom jewelry, earbuds, pocket crystals, special money (I recall a not-often-seen two-dollar bill!), angel figurines, and more.

I have a special soapstone carved figurine called Serenity that usually accompanies me on retreat. She holds space for me while I'm holding space for retreat participants. Having each person contribute to the altar helps their energy to fully show up in the sacred space and then when we complete the retreat, each participant collects her item during the closing circle. By taking that object back home with her, she's taking home a little bit of the magical energy we've stirred up during our time together. Each altar that we cocreate looks different and that's because what each of us considers sacred, grounded, and holy is so unique.

If you are going to build a personal altar, start by choosing an altar cloth which is often just a simple white cloth or a special cloth that is personal to you, perhaps a gift given by a friend or something you got from your travels that reminds you of a special place.

My favorite altar cloth is a gorgeous hand-quilted piece given to me by my virtual assistant, Ruth Martin. She knows my affinity for dragonflies (both my spirit animal and my Sacred Celebrations business logo), and one year as a surprise gift, she sent me the most gorgeous mini quilt with three different styles of quilting. It is truly a work of art and a treasured gift, and I immediately put it on my ancestral altar!

Here are some examples of items you can include on your altar(s):

- **Mother Earth**: rocks, sand, leaves, bark, flowers, shells, feathers
- **Sensory items**: candles, essential oils, incense, bells, beautiful fabric, or scarves
- **Art**: a child's drawing, pottery, mosaic, jewelry, poetry, photography
- **Spiritual items**: prayer beads, angels, statue of a beloved saint or goddess or deity, angel cards
- **Images**: photos or magazine cutouts of people, places, or sayings that inspire you—individually or collectively as a vision board

Keep in mind, an altar can begin very small with just one or two items and then expand as you get inspired with new items to place there. It is also important to periodically clean your altar. Pick up the items, dust them off and decide what remains and what needs to be removed. I find that I add to my altar every week or so as I find a new treasure—a pine cone, a feather, a favorite quote, a pocket crystal that appears in the jeans I haven't worn in seven months!

I have several altars in my home, but my favorite is my ancestral altar where I have photos of my parents and grandparents. It is where I go when I am seeking their wisdom and guidance.

Sometimes, I spend quite a bit of time talking out loud sharing my hopes and dreams, worries and anxieties. Other times, I simply sit quietly and listen for messages from them. And on busy days, I may just pass by and say, "Hi ancestors! Thank you for being here and watching over me and my family!" I take my mom offerings of white wine and licorice (her favorite candy), my dad offerings of vodka and Big Red chewing gum (his favorite), and I offer the grandparents different things like candies, chocolates, seeds, nuts, honey, and whatever feels inspired that particular day.

Chapter Twenty-One
Holidays

Take a deep breath and pause to reflect... What are some of your favorite holiday memories?

Do you recall going to the candlelight service on Christmas Eve with your family, saying grace around the Thanksgiving table, or celebrating the Hindu holiday Diwali, the festival of lights, with special sweet treats? Maybe you have created your own tradition of hosting an annual New Year's Eve party, treating your mom to brunch every year on Mother's Day, or honoring your spiritual well-being and the solemnity of Yom Kippur by fasting.

No matter where you live or what religion—if any—you practice, holidays are universal in society.

The etymology of the word comes from the Old English "holy days" and holidays were originally deemed for special religious celebrations. Over time, the meaning has expanded to include culturally or historically significant days as well. They are usually considered a day of rest and can include festivities that are not part of our normal routines. Think about drinking champagne on New

Year's, fireworks on Independence Day, and children dressing up in creative costumes for Halloween.

Holidays can be especially important in the life of a family because they help to strengthen ties and maintain connections. Holidays are often the only times that family members regularly take time to gather. Often members are scattered all over a city, around the country, or even live on different continents. But when everybody travels back home to the place where they all grew up, which can be especially meaningful if parents or grandparents still live there, sometimes it is just that once- or twice-a-year visit that is so critical to maintaining family relations. Being in person celebrating with relatives is often a deeper and richer experience than exchanging phone calls or letters from miles apart. During the COVID-19 pandemic, everyone had to find creative ways to adapt and connect meaningfully even while remaining virtual. It was an opportunity to think out of the box and reach for loved ones.

Holidays give us permission to slow down, take time off, and consciously and intentionally connect with people we love. Sometimes we are just grateful for a day or two off to either rest and relax or catch up on our long to-do list. Families may enjoy playing board games together, going for long walks, or spending hours together in the kitchen cooking favorite family recipes. Friends may enjoy gathering for a Friendsgiving potluck or plan an outdoor activity like hiking or biking if they are far away from or do not have family to connect with. Other people enjoy vacationing during the holidays to break tradition altogether.

Unlike some of the one-time events covered earlier in this book, holidays come around year after year after year. You may have grown up with traditions that were passed down from your parents and grandparents, or you may have created new traditions of your own.

In my husband's family, we have developed a tradition of renting a local gymnasium at Christmastime and playing "Minute to Win It" style games with the extended relatives (three siblings, their kids, and all the grandchildren). It has been a hilarious way to make lasting memories, especially for the youngest family members.

An avid cyclist friend of mine takes an annual New Year's Day bike ride with a close relative to kick off their new year doing something they're passionate about.

Remember that the holidays are not always stress-free for people. A variety of factors may lead to feeling sad, anxious, or lonely. Making modifications to traditions can help to ease the roller coaster of emotions.

- Losing a loved one and going through all the firsts without them can bring up a lot of grief. My mom died in September, so our first holiday without her was Thanksgiving. I didn't have the heart to prepare a home-cooked meal, so that year, we made reservations at a local restaurant. As luck would have it, they had lobster on the menu and lobster was one of my mom's favorite foods. So, I eschewed the traditional turkey meal in favor of enjoying lobster in honor of my mom.

- In families that have stepfamilies and multiple places to be, it can be exhausting running from one house to the next to the next to stuff in yet more holiday food. My Canadian friend Shauna shares joint custody of her two children with her ex-husband and his new wife. They've claimed Boxing Day (the day after Christmas) as the blended family day and that is sacred time that they all spend together.

- Finances can also be a concern for some people. If there is not enough money to travel, purchase gifts, or contribute to an elaborate meal, worries about money can be an added source of stress. This is why talking openly and honestly about expectations during the holidays is critical. Doing a white elephant gift exchange, giving only handmade gifts, or choosing a name out of a hat and buying a gift for only that one person can become fun traditions that people look forward to each year.

As you think about your own holiday gatherings, here are some fun and unique suggestions and ideas to infuse your festivities with more intention and meaning. For this list, we will focus on non-religious days of celebration, honoring, and remembrance.

New Year's Day—Create a vision board. Write intentions for the new year. Choose a word or theme for the year to guide your actions and discuss it with others. Eat black-eyed peas and collard greens to invite good luck (or choose a new prosperity-inducing meal!).

Martin Luther King, Jr. Day—Attend a parade in his honor. Read some of his writings with family or friends. Watch his historic "I Have a Dream" speech. Take a virtual tour of the National Civil Rights Museum in Memphis. Volunteer with an organization that is actively dismantling racism.

Valentine's Day—Encourage children to create handmade cards to give to family and friends. Prepare a special meal for loved ones. Take time at dinner to talk about the family's individual love languages (this is based on Gary Chapman's book *The Five Love Languages*).

Earth Day—Plant trees in the community. Pick up trash in the neighborhood. Teach children how to start a garden. Educate school or church members about ways they can recycle.

Memorial Day—Honor loved ones in the family who have died in the service by visiting their graves, telling stories, or looking at old photographs. Attend a Memorial Day service in the community. Teach children the difference between Memorial Day and Veterans Day.

Mother's/Father's Day—Make a list of all the reasons to appreciate parents or spouse. Encourage children to create art representing their love for their parents. Plan a surprise day of pampering or relaxation.

Chapter Twenty-One: Holidays

Juneteenth—Gather with friends and family at a cookout and discuss the importance of this significant day, commemorating the liberation of enslaved Black people in the US. Attend local parades, festivals, or protests. Visit a Black museum or cultural site or support Black organizations in your community.

Independence Day—Review the history lesson of how this (or any other) country was founded. Visit a patriotic landmark. Design an Independence Day trivia quiz to share at a neighborhood picnic or barbecue. Talk with the children about the freedoms we experience living in a democracy.

Halloween/Day of the Dead—Create an altar to honor the ancestors. Include photos, flowers, and offerings of food and drink. Tell stories about ancestors. Research the family genealogy to learn more about them.

Thanksgiving—At the dinner table, invite each person to express gratitude out loud. Volunteer at a food pantry. Honor Native American communities by learning about a given area and discussing the true history of colonization in the US.

Religious holidays like Easter, Passover, Ramadan, Rosh Hashanah, Yom Kippur, Hanukkah, Christmas, and many others have a whole host of their own ceremonies and traditions. Many have grown up observing certain rituals year after year with their family or community. When people of two different faith traditions marry, both traditions can be melded into the newly formed family. My brother-in-law is Jewish, and my sister-in-law is Christian, so they are raising their three daughters to celebrate and honor both traditions at home.

Cultural holidays are also important in the life of a family, and if there isn't much about the ancestors' festivities, a little research will go a long way in creating traditions that will bring meaning and joy. Some other holidays from different cultures and traditions include but are not limited to Chinese New Year, Mardi Gras, St. Patrick's Day, Holi, Bastille Day, Kwanzaa, and Boxing Day.

Celebrating some of the more modern along with made-up holidays like Groundhog Day, Galantine's Day, Grandparents Day, and others can add more playfulness and joy to the world.

Many have a newly acquired interest in their ancestors because of genetic DNA testing sites like Ancestry.com or 23andme.com. It can be fun to learn about traditions that your ancestors may have celebrated and bring them into your modern-day experience. Families who have adopted children from another culture, country, or race may want to be especially mindful of this as well. In recent years, through reunion with her paternal biological family, we learned that our adopted daughter has a Mexican grandfather and Japanese great-grandparents. As a result, we are learning a bit more about both of those cultures to support her in understanding her roots better.

Chapter Twenty-Two
Cycles of Nature

"In the relentless busyness of modern life, we have lost the rhythm between work and rest… And for want of rest, our lives are in danger." Wayne Muller opens his book *Sabbath: Finding Rest, Renewal and Delight in our Daily Lives* with these words, which is a powerful message we should all listen to.[53]

Our lives are in danger.

Wow. Just sit with that for a minute.

We must reconnect with nature and Mother Earth if we are to reconnect to ourselves. We come from the stars and our bodies return to dust once we pass from this earthly life. But while we are here, living more consciously in tune with the cycles and the seasons makes for a more harmonious way of living, not only for ourselves but for other humans, animals, and plants that inhabit the earth.

One of the many reasons I wrote this book is because I am passionate about our absolute need to reunite with ourselves, others, and with Spirit. We have become so distracted, disembodied, and disconnected we have lost our capacity to follow the innate rhythms of our human design.

Electricity beckons us to stay up later reading, watching television, surfing our devices, or getting lost in video games instead of listening to the inner rhythms which would invite us to quietly read a book, snuggle with our children, make love to a partner, or simply go to sleep earlier because our bodies require rest.

If we tune in to Mother Nature's natural rhythms, we will see that we have many opportunities for rebalancing rituals daily, monthly, and seasonally. Connecting intentionally with the sun, the moon, and the change of seasons is good for our health and well-being. Exposure to morning natural light can help to regulate our hormones and promote healthy sleep. Walking in the moonlight can help to offload any residual stress from a busy day's activities. Ayurvedic and Traditional Chinese Medicine suggest that modifying eating habits and other self-care practices in synchronicity with the change of seasons supports our physical, emotional, and spiritual wellness.

Every day, twice a day, Mother Nature gives us a dazzling show of beauty. Taking time to watch the sunrise or sunset is an opportunity to pause and contemplate the transitions that we go through every single day from rest to activity and back to rest. The sunrise is an opportunity to be filled with possibility and promise about the new day that is dawning.

Early morning liminal space is a wonderful time for prayer, meditation, and peaceful contemplation. One of my coaching clients is a personal trainer who gets up in the wee hours of the morning to lead an outdoor boot camp training program several times a week. She will sometimes leave me a video message via Marco Polo and invariably she'll get quiet from her ramblings and pause for a few moments to show me the awe-inspiring sunrise. Even though she experiences it daily, it never gets old and leaves her speechless for just a little bit.

Conversely, at the end of the day, carving out a few minutes to pause activities and watch the setting sun fade into the landscape is a great way to shift from the action-oriented yang energy of the day to the gentler, more feminine yin energy of the evening.

As a child growing up in Connecticut, we vacationed regularly in Florida because my grandparents lived there. I distinctly remember most evenings we would sit outside for the sacred ritual of happy hour, drink cocktails (wine and spirits for the grown-ups and usually a Shirley Temple or some Orange Crush for me), nibble on hors d'oeuvres, and watch the sunset. We would talk and laugh and play shuffleboard in my grandparents' backyard, and we would recount the activities of the day and what fun we had together as a family. It was a distinct transition period from the busy nature of the day to the more relaxed pace of the evening.

The monthly moon cycles impact the earth with changes in light and changes in the tides. Animal navigation, migration, and reproduction often correlate with the cycles of the moon, and high and low tide in the ocean are orchestrated by the moon's gravitational pull on the earth.

In the art and science of astrology, the new moon is considered a great time for setting intentions and goals and for planting seeds of ideas and things we want to manifest in our lives. When the full moon returns each month, it is a great time for releasing that which no longer serves us and letting go of any thoughts, beliefs, and emotions that might be holding us back from living our fullest potential.

The changes of the seasons are marked by solstices and equinoxes. In the Northern Hemisphere, the summer solstice, the longest day of the year, occurs in June and the winter solstice, the shortest day of the year, occurs in December. These are when the Sun's path in the sky is farthest from the equator.

Years ago, when I first lived in the mountains, a group of friends created a tradition to go for a long summer solstice hike every June.

It was usually a full-day affair that invited us to be outside soaking up the sunshine and fresh mountain air. Winter solstice rituals can include turning off electricity and embracing the darkness, perhaps only lighting candles or a fire, to really embrace the entrance into winter. It is an excellent time to write out anything we are ready to release—anger, frustration, resentment—and then burn it! It is a powerful letting-go ritual that can be done any time of year but lines up beautifully with the letting-go energy of the winter solstice.

The spring equinox occurs in March and the fall equinox occurs in September, and those are when the Sun is directly above the equator so that daytime and nighttime are of equal length. Spring cleaning and decluttering are popular activities to do around the spring equinox. If you have children in your life, it's also a great time to plant a garden, decorate eggs, play in the mud, or host a spring-themed party. The fall equinox can be celebrated by visiting a local farm or farmer's market, preparing a fall-themed meal, or decorating your home with autumnal touches. It's also a great time for a gratitude ritual, spoken or written, to celebrate the harvest of all that is good in your life.

In traditional Western culture, farmers are still deeply connected to and impacted by the seasons. And anyone who gardens, even if a small plot of land in their backyard, also is more in touch with the natural cycles of life. Winter is for hibernation, spring for planting, summer for growth, and fall for harvest.

If you want to be more conscious and intentional about connecting with the cycles of Mother Nature, consider adding the following rituals to your daily life:

- Choose to wake up early and watch the sunrise.
- Design your schedule so that you can take a break between work and evening time to watch the sunset.
- Mark your calendar for the new moon and plan to set monthly goals or intentions around that day.

- Note when the full moon occurs each month and plan to go for an evening walk in the moonlight, charge moon water or your crystals, or hold hands with a lover as you soak up the magical moonbeams.

- Celebrate the seasons by planning a solstice or equinox ritual alone or with loved ones. This can be a great opportunity to teach children about the change of seasons.

Conclusion
The World Needs More Rituals

Hopefully you are feeling inspired, uplifted, and filled with ideas. Celebration (and commemoration) is both an art and a science that can be incorporated into life easily if you explore it with curiosity and creativity. There's no right or wrong way to do this; simply allow your intuition to guide you.

What ritual do you want to do first? When can you do it? Perhaps you have a big life transition coming up and you are excited to implement some of the concepts in the earlier chapters. Or maybe you love the idea of simple daily rituals that infuse your life with more magic and meaning. Whichever it is, don't wait.

Some rituals you could do right away:

- Establish a morning ritual of sitting for ten minutes outside with your cup of tea.
- Begin a weekly gratitude ritual with your beloveds at Sunday night family dinner.
- Plan for three months of date nights with your partner and watch your connection grow.

- Set aside time each day to pray at your new home altar.
- Become aware of the cycles of Mother Nature and commit to tuning in to her natural rhythms of the sun and moon.

In my twenty-plus years of experience as a coach and entrepreneur, I have found that it is critical to follow the inspiration muse when she strikes. If you get an idea that really fires you up, start taking action on it immediately. Or, if you can't do that, at least write it down and capture it so you can revisit your intuitive hits when the time is right.

My sincere hope is that you, dear reader, will find a way to enrich all aspects of your life—spiritual, emotional, mental, and physical—with the ritual ideas that were presented in this book. All of life is evolution. Change goes in cycles with distinct stages of beginning, transformation, maturation, and completion. Everything is born and then dies, and then cycles begin all over again. We experience thousands of beginnings and endings, day after day and year after year.

Also, you might have noticed most of the ideas presented in this book were designed with community in mind. Rituals bring us together and bond us more closely, making us more resilient and better able to thrive. So why not discuss these ideas with your supper club? Introduce some of the concepts to your coworkers or employees. Engage your family at the dinner table with questions about their daily rituals and what they believe to be sacred. Get your book club to read this book together and then cocreate a ritual as a group.

Just like the pebble dropped into the pond, the impact of the ripple effect when you share an idea with others can help spark growth and evolution for many. My wish is that this book will be passed down from generation to generation, reminding us of the connections we share and the sacredness of ritual in all stages of our lives.

With each new cycle, may we breathe deeper, love harder, forgive more readily, and expand our minds further.

With love and gratitude,

Elizabeth

Asheville, North Carolina, Fall 2023

Let's Stay Connected!

Now you have a more comprehensive understanding of the value of Sacred Celebrations and how rituals can enhance your life in beautiful ways. The best way to incorporate creative ideas and create new routines that support your mind, body and spirit is to engage with others regularly who are on a similar path. I invite you to become part of my world and let's learn and grow together!

- Join my Facebook group Sacred Celebrations
  www.facebook.com/groups/sacredcelebrations
- Follow me on Facebook
  www.facebook.com/sacredcelebrationsgifts
- Follow me on Instagram
  www.instagram.com/sacredcelebrationsgifts and
  www.instagram.com/elizabthbarbour
- Email me to tell me about your Sacred Celebrations. I love hearing your stories! info@sacredcelebrations.com
- I'd love to speak at your group or women's organization
  www.elizabethbarbour.com/speaking
- I'd love to be a guest on your podcast, radio, or TV show!

Acknowledgments

"It takes a village" is so cliché… but it's so darned true! Writing a book is a labor of love. There are so many people who helped to midwife this baby into being… I'll apologize now if I miss acknowledging somebody but know that if you're in my life, chances are good you helped me at some point along the way and for that, I am eternally grateful.

Let me start with the coaching support I've received over the years. I'm grateful to Christine Closer's *Get Your Book Done* program for helping me start this project with practical to-dos and a real-world understanding of what it takes to write and publish a book. Lynne Klippel was an extraordinary book coach to me for more than a year as I wrestled with the visioning of this book, the discipline of writing, and moving past all my inner gremlins that tried to sabotage this project. Just one session with Hayley Foster was a huge parting-of-the-heavens-and-angels-singing moment that allowed the form to crystallize and take shape and set me on the trajectory for what you now hold in your hands.

Sarah Bamford Seidelmann not only wrote the foreword (thank youuuuuuuu dearest Sarah for helping introduce this work to the world!) but was also instrumental in getting me to ask for help in the early stages. I was stuck on the idea that I'm a coach and speaker but not a writer, yet I also insisted I didn't want a ghostwriter; I wanted to do it myself—stubborn entrepreneur that I am! She introduced the idea of a developmental editor to me, and my shoulders immediately relaxed when I realized I didn't have to finish writing all alone.

Dawn Ius was the first developmental editor that I worked with, and her weekly accountability and insightful questions helped get

Acknowledgements

my ideas out of my head and onto the page which was a monumental struggle.

Then Shauna Hardy with the GracePoint team lovingly held the big vision of this book while also holding my hand across the finish line as I encountered all sorts of personal health and family challenges in the final year of bringing this book to life. Her belief in this message never faltered, even when I did.

The rest of the team at GracePoint were rockstars, too. Karen Curry Parker, Michelle Vandepas, Tascha Yoder, and Laurie Knight have all offered invaluable input, support, and encouragement. Their commitment to collaboration and conscious change is making the world a better place, and I'm delighted to be part of their vision.

Extra special thanks to all the people who agreed to let me share their celebrations and rituals in this book. Several people allowed me to interview them, and others answered my questions on Facebook and allowed me to share their anecdotes and personal stories.

My writing mastermind group deserves special mention for creating an intellectual and inspirational container to help hold me accountable in moving this project forward inch by inch: Jon, Ceal, Robin, and especially Danielle Metcalf-Chenail, who has been one of my main cheerleaders, an inspiring leader, and a cherished friend.

Colleen O'Grady, my friend and colleague, has been about five years ahead of me in her own process of writing and publishing and has changed thousands of lives because of her work. She's shared her rollercoaster journey with me, and I've been in awe of her success. Thanks for modeling the pathway... now it's my turn and thanks for cheering me on!

I am blessed to have some of the dearest friends that one could ever ask for: besties until the end in Whitney, Bean and Joe, my FR girlfriends, the Houston mom friends, my coaching mastermind buddies, and too many others to name. My family members (through adoption, birth, and marriage!) are always loving and supportive, and I am grateful for all of them!

Most of all, a deep debt of gratitude to Eric, for always seeing the best in me and believing that I could write this book. It's finally done. You don't have to hear me fuss about it anymore! What a journey we've had together over two decades. Being family with you and Roo is one of the best things to ever happen to me.

xo, E.

Notes

Chapter 4

1. Friedman, H. and Martin, L. (2011) *The Longevity Project: Surprising Discoveries for Health and Long Life from the Landmark Eight-Decade Study.* New York: Hudson Street Press.

2. Cigna. (2020) "Loneliness and the Workplace" [Infographic]. Cigna.com. cigna-2020-loneliness-infographic.pdf

3. "Loneliness in America: How the Pandemic Has Deepened an Epidemic of Loneliness and What We Can Do About It." (2021, February) *Making Caring Common Harvard Graduate School of Education.* https://mcc.gse.harvard.edu/reports/loneliness-in-america

4. Curtin, M. (2019, Feb 11) "25 Oprah Winfrey Quotes That Will Empower You (and Make You Laugh)." *Inc.* https://www.inc.com/melanie-curtin/25-oprah-winfrey-quotes-that-will-empower-you-and-make-you-laugh.html

Chapter 5

5. "Fast Facts: Preventing Adverse Childhood Experiences." (2022, April 22) *CDC* https://www.cdc.gov/violenceprevention/aces/fastfact.html

6. "Essential Guide To Serotonin And The Other Happy Hormones In Your Body." (2022, May 27) *Atlas Biomed.* https://atlasbiomed.com/blog/serotonin-and-other-happy-molecules-made-by-gut-bacteria/

Notes

Chapter 7

7. Tillman, N. (2010) *On the Night You Were Born*. New York: Feiwel & Friends.

8. Van Luling, T. (2017, December 6) "This Is Why You Get To Celebrate Your Birthday Every Year" *HuffPost* https://www.huffpost.com/entry/history-of-birthdays_n_4227366

9. Ruiz, D. M. (1997) *The Four Agreements: A Practical Guide to Personal Freedom* (A Toltec Wisdom Book) California: Amber-Allen Publishing.

10. "7 Cultures That Celebrate Aging And Respect Their Elders." (2017, Dec 6) *HuffPost* https://www.huffpost.com/entry/what-other-cultures-can-teach_n_4834228

Chapter 8

11. Nunez, C. and Pfeffer, L. (2016, July 21) "13 Amazing Coming of Age Traditions From Around the World." *Global Citizen.* https://www.globalcitizen.org/en/content/13-amazing-coming-of-age-traditions-from-around-th/

Chapter 9

12. Herman, Jane. (2022) "12 Rituals You May See at a Jewish Wedding." *ReformJudaism.org.* https://reformjudaism.org/beliefs-practices/lifecycle-rituals/weddings/12-rituals-you-may-see-jewish-wedding

13. Schaer, R.B. (2022) "Quaker Ceremony Wedding Rituals." *TheKnot.com.* https://www.theknot.com/content/quaker-wedding-ceremony-rituals

14. Montemayor, C. (2021, Dec 20) "Everything You Need to Know About the Wedding Lasso Tradition." *Brides.com.* https://www.brides.com/wedding-lasso-5074699#

15. "Discover The Most Intriguing African Wedding Traditions." (2020, June 23) *Jo Sa Bi Marie'es.* https://www.josabimariees.com/tips/discover-african-wedding-traditions/

16. Labarrie, A. (2021, Dec 20) "Everything You Need to Know About the Libation Ceremony." Brides*.com.* https://www.brides.com/libation-ceremony-5079929#

Chapter 10

17. Linn, D. (1995) *Sacred Space: Clearing and Enhancing the Energy of Your Home.* Canada: Wellspring/Ballantine.

18. Bright Hub Education. (2011, June 30) "Traditional Use of the Housewarming Blessing: A Look at Various Housewarming Traditions" https://www.brighthubeducation.com/social-studies-help/120751-the-house-warming-tradition-and-blessing-in-cultures/

19. Hensrud, S. (2015, Sept) "You Should Go to a Habitat for Humanity Dedication!" *HomesMSP.* https://homesmsp.com/2014/09/habitat-for-humanity-dedication.html

Chapter 11

20. The American Institute of Stress. (2022) "The Holmes-Rae Stress Inventory." https://www.stress.org/holmes-rahe-stress-inventory

21. Miller, A. (2013, April) "Can This Marriage Be Saved?" *American Psychological Association.* https://www.apa.org/monitor/2013/04/marriage#

22. Ellin, Abby. (2012, April 29) "Leaving A Spouse Behind. For Good." *New York Times.* https://www.nytimes.com/2012/04/29/fashion/weddings/leaving-a-spouse-behind-for-good.html

23. Public Delivery. (2022, June 18). "Marina Abramović walks China's Great Wall only to break up." https://publicdelivery.org/marina-abramovic-the-lovers-the-great-wall-walk/

24. Perel, Esther. (2018) *The State of Affairs: Rethinking Infidelity.* New York: HarperCollins.

25. Thomas, K.W. (2016) *Conscious Uncoupling: 5 Steps to Living Happily Even After.* New York: Harmony.

26. Danielson, Julie. (2015, December 18) "It's Time to Celebrate Divorce." *Scary Mommy.* https://www.scarymommy.com/its-time-to-celebrate-divorce

Chapter 12

27. Kübler-Ross, E. (2014). *On Death and Dying: What the Dying Have to Teach Doctors, Nurses, Clergy and Their Own Families.* New York: Scribner.

Notes

28. Painter, S. (2022) "Mourning Band History and Common Protocols." *Love to Know*. https://dying.lovetoknow.com/about-obituaries-memorials/mourning-band-history-common-protocols

29. *Funeral Wise*. (2022) "Jewish Funeral Service Rituals." https://www.funeralwise.com/funeral-customs/jewish/

30. Cellania, M. (2016, May 30) "Why Are Flowers Placed on Graves?" https://www.neatorama.com/2016/05/30/Why-Are-Flowers-Placed-on-Graves/

31. *Funeral Wise*. (2022) "Funeral Customs." https://www.funeralwise.com/funeral-customs/

32. *Cremation Institute* (2022) "Muslim Funeral Traditions: 10 Things You Should Know" https://cremationinstitute.com/muslim-funeral-traditions/

33. *Funeral Partners*. (2022) "Hindu Funerals." https://www.funeralpartners.co.uk/help-advice/arranging-a-funeral/types-of-funerals/hindu-funeral-rites-and-death-rituals/

34. Tretrault, S. (2022, May 15) "What Happens at an Irish Wake: Customs, Songs & Etiquette." *Joincake* (blog). https://www.joincake.com/blog/irish-wake/#

35. *National Museum of Funeral History*. (2022) "Jazz Funerals of New Orleans." https://www.nmfh.org/portfolio-item/jazz-funerals-of-new-orleans/

36. Stone, Bradley. (2020, April 17) "7 Compelling Reasons Why a "Living Funeral" Can Make Your Final Moments Beautiful." *Medium*. https://medium.com/all-about-surrounding/7-compelling-reasons-why-a-living-funeral-can-make-your-final-moments-beautiful-75ccf90ae49b

37. Kim, E.K. (2016, August 18) "Woman with ALS throws 'rebirth' party before ending her life." *Today*. https://www.today.com/health/woman-als-throws-rebirth-party-ending-her-life-t101869

38. Rockafellow, M. (2020, May 19) "Coins left on cemetery headstones have meaning." *Vilas County News-Review*. https://vcnewsreview.com/Content/Default/OPINION/Article/Coins-left-on-cemetery-headstones-have-meaning/-3/1223/228518#

39. *History.com.* (2009, November 24) "Archaeologist opens tomb of King Tut." https://www.history.com/this-day-in-history/archaeologist-opens-tomb-of-king-tut

40. Katz, J. (2012) *Going Home: Finding Peace When Pets Die.* New York: Random House.

Chapter 13

41. Bisaria, A. (2018, January 21). "11 First Period Traditions From Around The World That Celebrate A Girl's Journey Into Womanhood." *India Times.* https://www.indiatimes.com/culture/11-first-period-traditions-from-around-the-world-that-celebrate-a-girl-s-journey-into-womanhood-338129.html

42. Mansfield, E. (1992) "Gathering in the Gorge." https://elainemansfield.com/womens-health/gathering-in-the-gorge-a-menopause-ritual/

Chapter 14

43. Brown, B. (2015) *Daring Greatly: How the Courage to Be Vulnerable Transforms the Way We Live, Love, Parent, and Lead.* New York: Avery.

Chapter 15

44. Schultz, H. (1997) *Pour Your Heart Into It: How Starbucks Built a Company One Cup at a Time.* Connecticut: Hyperion.

45. Warrillow, J. (2010, Dec 20) "The Secret Rituals and Traditions That Bring Teams Together" *CBS News.* https://www.cbsnews.com/news/the-secret-rituals-and-traditions-that-bring-teams-together/

46. Liu, V. (2017, June 6) "The song-and-exercise routines of the modern Chinese workplace have revolutionary roots." *Quartz.* https://qz.com/996047/the-song-and-exercise-morning-routines-of-modern-chinese-offices-have-revolutionary-roots/

Chapter 16

47. Adams, B. (2017, September 7*)* "6 Morning Rituals of Steve Jobs, Tony Robbins, Oprah, and Other Successful Leaders." *Inc.* https://www.inc.com/bryan-adams/6-celebrity-morning-rituals-to-help-you-kick-ass.html

Notes

48. Deyan G. (2022, June 2) "How Much Time Do People Spend on Social Media in 2022?" *Tech Jury.* https://techjury.net/blog/time-spent-on-social-media/#gref

49. Ackerman, C.E. (2017, April 12) "28 Benefits of Gratitude & Most Significant Research Findings." *Positive Psychology.* https://positivepsychology.com/benefits-gratitude-research-questions/

Chapter 17

50. Dyer, W. (2009, Oct 15) "Success Secrets." https://www.drwaynedyer.com/blog/success-secrets/

Chapter 19

51. Buchholz, K. (2021, April 3) "Where Daily Prayer is Most Common." *Statista.* https://www.statista.com/chart/17865/daily-prayer-worldwide/

Chapter 20

52. Dyer, W. (1989) You'll See It When You Believe It: The Way to Your Personal Transformation. New York: William and Morrow.

Chapter 22

53. Muller, W. (2000) *Sabbath: Finding Rest, Renewal and Delight in our Daily Lives.* New York: Random House.

Resources

Books

Albom, Mitch. (1992) *Tuesdays with Morrie*. New York: Crown.

Gilbert, Elizabeth. (2006) *Eat Pray Love*. New York: Riverhead Books.

Kübler-Ross, Elisabeth and Kessler, David. (2005) *On Grief and Grieving*. New York: Scribner.

Lamott, Anne. (2012) *Help, Thanks, Wow: The Three Essential Prayers*. New York: Riverhead Books.

Linn, Denise. (1995) *Sacred Space: Clearing and Enhancing the Energy in Your Home*. New York: Wellspring/Ballantine.

McTaggart, Lynne. (2017) *The Power of Eight: Harnessing the Miraculous Energies of a Small Group to Heal Others, Your Life, and the World*. New York: Atria.

Muller, Wayne. (2000) *Sabbath: Finding Rest, Renewal and Delight in Our Busy Lives*. New York: Random House.

Thomas, Katherine Woodward. (2016) *Conscious Uncoupling: 5 Steps to Living Happily Even After*. New York: Harmony.

Videos

First Moon Party by Hello Flo
https://www.youtube.com/watch?v=NEcZmT0fiNM&t=2s

Period. End of Sentence.
https://www.youtube.com/watch?v=Lrm2pD0qofM

Elizabeth Barbour

Elizabeth Barbour graduated from William & Mary with degrees in biology and psychology, but along the way through personal triumph and tragedy, discovered ritual was her passion and the best pathway to navigate this crazy rollercoaster of life. For more than two decades, she has helped her clients live more magical and meaningful lives as an intuitive life and business coach and shamanic practitioner. She is a creative force when to comes to releasing pain, healing wounds, transforming old stories into new beginnings, and celebrating the beauty and joy of life's milestones.

For the past twenty years, rituals have been a cornerstone of Elizabeth Barbour's life. From beating her furniture with a tennis racket to release the anger at her ex-husband, to conducting a heartfelt white rose ceremony at her mother's memorial, she uses rituals to navigate, heal, celebrate, and connect deeply to her own life. She is devoted to helping people unearth the beauty and sacredness of their lives and she helps make ritual accessible for everyone.

Barbour lives in the majestic mountains of Asheville, North Carolina with her family (both human and four-legged) and oodles of soulmate friends.

She is also the author of *Smart Self-Care for Busy Women: 20 Lessons for the Me Time That You Crave.*

Find out more at www.elizabethbarbour.com

For more great books from Empower Press
Visit Books.GracePointPublishing.com

If you enjoyed reading *Sacred Celebrations*, and purchased it through an online retailer, please return to the site and write a review to help others find the book

www.ingramcontent.com/pod-product-compliance
Lightning Source LLC
Chambersburg PA
CBHW020050170426
43199CB00009B/235